I QUIT

AND CHOOSE WORK THAT ALIGNS WITH MY SOUL

Karyn Pettigrew

Copyright © 2002 by Karyn Kerr Pettigrew

Published and distributed in the United States by KPConsulting, 1803 W. 95th Street, P.O.Box 116, Chicago, Illinois 60643 • Phone (773) 233-9214 • Karyn@kpconsulting.biz

Editorial Supervision: Bruce Clorfene

Author's Photograph: Josh Dreyfus

Cover Photo: ©Gabriela Medina/Superstock, Inc

The author of this book does not dispense medical advice or prescribe the use of any technique as a form of treatment for physical or medical problems without the advice of a physician, either directly or indirectly. The intent of the author is to offer information of a general nature to help you in pursuing intellectual, emotional and spiritual well-being. In the event that you use any of the information in this book for yourself, which is your right, the author and the publisher assume no responsibility for your actions.

ISBN 0-9746087-0-X

This book is dedicated to those courageous beings who sense that it is time for a change and are willing to do something about it.

Acknowledgements

Thanks to God and my Guides for walking with me every moment; to the clients, students and friends whose stories help to illustrate and enrich the messages in this book; to my husband Carl, for finding the courage to support my leap; to my children Cameron and Nick for helping to keep me grounded and reminding me to laugh; to my soul sisters, Bernice—my Mom, Kristyn and Sandra for their unfailing support; to my earth angels Sonia Choquette for being a master teacher and offering her mirror to me; Desiree Rogers for being what I needed, when I needed it; Jeff Schweig for believing, seeing and guiding me; Kurt Hill for leading me to invaluable information and helping me call my spirit back.

TABLE OF CONTENTS

I QUIT

SECTION ONE

What is this book?

INTRODUCTION

This book is my attempt to help bring greater harmony to the planet one person at a time. I do not believe that sweeping military action, national legislation, or financial coercion will bring peace. I believe that peace will unfold more like a chain of dominoes, person-by-person, where each has chosen to live for the joy in his life, focusing on work, and in doing so, inspire another to do the same.

Imagine a symphony. A flute played by itself is beautiful, but if we add a violin and then a French horn, the energy and magnificence of the music grows. As we continue to add instruments, each contributes a unique tone, until we have a full, harmonious sound, unattainable with any one instrument alone. I believe that harmony on our planet will occur this way as well. It will not come from one church, one leader, or one message. Just as there are thousands of languages, there will be many human catalysts that encourage others to find their paths. We all have a preferred method of learning and preferred teachers, but whatever the form, by introducing principles that will yield greater personal harmony, there will be an extrapolation of healing to the global level.

I believe that we can begin to experience greater personal satisfaction by choosing to do work that aligns with our truest nature, our soul. I have written *I Quit and choose work that aligns with my soul* to offer up one additional instrument in the global healing orchestra.

Karyn Pettigrew

This book is organized into six sections. The first section, "**What is this book**?" presents the background for the book. I share my observations regarding what is happening in our work environments to make a book of this type necessary. I lay out what I think it will take to help bring relief to the discomfort that so many people are experiencing in their lives.

Section 2. "Choosing work that aligns with your soul," explains that you must first know who you are, how you define yourself, and what you want in your life before you can move toward a more balanced, joyful work experience. I use my own experience and those of my students and clients to highlight the concepts.

Section 3. "Where to begin?" presents the principles of truth, trust and responsibility. You must be willing to embrace them before you can create the life and thereby the work that aligns with your soul.

Section 4. "Looking at yourself," begins your personal assessment. Through reflective questions, guided meditations and thoughtful exercises, you will clarify your priorities in each of four aspects--your intellectual self, your physical self, your emotional self, and your spiritual self. Ultimately, this clarification will allow you to better discern the steps necessary to create the life and work you desire.

Section 5. "Making it happen" presents principles for honoring and manifesting your dreams. These principles ask you to reclaim your vital resources and restore your power. Creating and living your vision requires the elimination of as many wasteful uses of your resources as possible. The exercises and questions offered in this section will help you to identify personal distractions such as complaining, blaming, and working without inspiration.

I QUIT

Section 6. "Epilogue – my personal journey" is a series of excerpts from my personal journal. It's a frank expression of my experiences in the moment. Sometimes, just hearing another's story is enough to remind us that we are not alone on this journey, and may inspire us to push on.

Journal Entry 1/5/02

Yesterday I quit my job. Well, actually I gave notice that I would be leaving in March. It was a much anticipated and agonizing decision. The conversation was great, but the process has been painful over the past few months. I do believe that I needed to be that uncomfortable in order to make the decision that I finally made. There were times before I announced when I felt like, "hum, it's not so bad. I could do this a while longer," and then I'd get a flair up and "remember" how stressful my job could be. Then again, I know (intellectually) that no one can make me feel anything. I have to allow it. I wonder if I quit because I was afraid of failing in a new position. But I'd only fail because it wasn't the right place for me. So, no, all of my cues signal my next act. I feel workshops, presentations, motivational speaking. I want to re-light the fire in people's hearts. Right now, I feel a little relieved, not anxious or afraid. I am trusting, really trusting my heart that this is right. I expect there to be further clarity regarding my "next step." I expect to be guided to the next step. I have surrendered and I am open. I feel like I just need to "be," and to be aware.

And so begins the journey. You already know that the time for change is now. It is the very reason you are reading this book.

I QUIT

WHY THIS BOOK, NOW?

"A new socioquake transforms mainstream America and the world as the pillars of society are questioned and rejected."
Icon Tumbling – Emerging trend
Faith Popcorn, *The Popcorn Report*

We are in the midst of an enormous global change. The leadership in our corporations, organizations, political parties and special interest groups are no longer guaranteed the unquestioned loyalty of their membership. Groupthink, or Zeitgeist, is evolving and bringing forth the realization of our individual natures in the midst of our collective participation on earth. *We* and *I* are the same. The agencies and organizations that took on a fiduciary responsibility for our well-being; our government, social service agencies, churches and schools are stretched, swollen, and cracking in an attempt to meet the needs of an increasingly diverse population. Old paradigms are coming undone.

. I believe that many of the dramatic, negative, socio-political events occurring today are symbolic demonstrations of the need for us to look closely at ourselves and our beliefs. We are being signaled to rethink what it means to be responsible for ourselves. We are being asked to review our relationship to victim-hood. We are being asked to take charge of our own lives.

At one time, the federal government, our churches, our schools, and even our employers could be considered our personal safety nets. Today, we are confronted with the limitations of that paradigm. Insufficient funding of programs such as social security or Medicare, allegations of sexual abuse in the Catholic church,

Karyn Pettigrew

corporate fraud and misconduct, metal detectors in our schools, and cyclical layoffs all demonstrate a need for us to rethink the goals and priorities in our lives. We must see our true selves and take responsibility for the life that we want to live. Organizations or other people are not the best sources for clarifying who we are, nor should we rely on them to direct our lives. This book will guide you to look inside. Re-discover your true desires through exercises that are powerful, yet easy to follow. This is an opportunity to follow your heart through to the message and the life that is meant just for you.

WHAT'S HAPPENING TO US?

The greatest challenge facing us is not survival in the traditional sense of food, clothing, and shelter. The world produces sufficient resources to provide basic necessities to all who need it. The question is why those resources are hoarded, burnt, or withheld to create scarcity? I believe that we are driven by our desire for power and perceived control. One of the greatest myths is that access to personal power lies outside of us, and that the way to have true power is through the acquisition of things, titles, money, or status. As we quest externally for this power, we *aspire toward affluence.*

This aspiration is the reason why so many people are workaholics. We long to keep up, to feel equal. Today, we have more of everything. So, the end appears to justify the means. However, we are not aspiring from a place that will result in our best. An aspiration based on comparing *"how well we look relative to anyone else"* comes from ego. When we come from ego, we sell ourselves short. Trying to be as good as someone else, instead of being all that we are capable of being, limits our unique individual expression. It limits our gift, our personal imprint on humanity.

Today, we have doubled the potential for discomfort in our lives. How well we are doing is not only measured by the things we acquire–house, car, clothes, and title-but also by how we place demands on our time. In a perverse way, we wear our hectic schedules like a badge of honor. We somehow validate our membership in society when we are paged on the train, "located" on our cell phones, "call in" from vacation, or complain about being a shuttle service for our children. We have become entangled, over-identified, and over-committed to the work we do. No job is immune.

Don, a friend of mine, used to complain incessantly of always feeling at the beck-and-call of his boss. Work was a constant presence in his life. Even on family vacations he would participate in conference calls or spend hours working out urgent client issues. When his wife challenged him about whether others in his office worked this way, he told her that it was "standard" practice for the partners in the firm.

Unfortunately, we are normalizing ourselves to this accelerated lifestyle. We are even scheduling our children down to the minute – soccer, baseball, gymnastics, dancing, music, art class. Again, in a perverse way, it feels like we are dropping the ball if we do not do it. Test yourself.

- Think about declining the request for your voluntary participation at church, school, or another not-for-profit board.
- Think about not calling in on vacation.
- Think about spending your entire Saturday afternoon on the couch.
- Think about not going to another company-sponsored event.

Do you feel resistance? What do you want to do about it?

HOW HAS MY LIFE CHANGED?

Sometimes we forget that we are part of the stream of consciousness we call life. We often go about things the same way for years. Have you noticed how your life has changed? Complete the following exercise to begin to explore the shifts that have occurred in your life.

Priorities Today	Priorities Ten Years Ago
1._____	1. _____
_____	_____
_____	_____
2._____	2. _____
_____	_____
_____	_____
3._____	3. _____
_____	_____
_____	_____

How do you feel about the shift? Did you notice it? What changes have occurred in your life as a result of your current priorities?

HOW DO YOU SPEND YOUR TIME DAILY?

Personal: Fun, self-directed, your willing decision
Work: Tasks you engage in regularly, daily.
Other: Less than complete willingness to participate,
             coercion, "if you don't, no one else will"
             activities.

% Personal_____   % Work _____   % Other _____

HOW WOULD YOU PREFER
TO SPEND YOUR TIME DAILY?

% Personal_____   % Work _____   % Other _____

How do you feel about the way you spend your time versus how you'd prefer spending your time? What prevents you from spending your time the way you'd prefer? Begin to think about what things may need to change to support your preference.

HAVE YOU BEEN BODY-SNATCHED?

Remember the 1950's movie, *Invasion of the Body Snatchers?* In the movie, an alien species comes to take over the Earth. They clone people and in the process remove the person's self-determination, free-will, and choice. The clone proceeds to "go through the motions" of the person's life. Because the clone so closely resembles the person physically, friends and family are slow to detect the switch. All of the changes were internal.

It's just a movie and it may sound ridiculous. But do you feel like you're just "going through the motions" day after day? Is your internal person different today? Do you feel as though your vitality, your essence has evaporated? Many of us have been body-snatched. Even if we notice it, we rarely know what to do about it.

Technology has made our lives easier, but it has also blurred the lines between home and work. It has provided employers, or other significant "owners" of our time, with virtually intravenous access to us via pagers, e-mail, facsimiles, and cell-phones. What it means to work in today's society has changed significantly over the last decade. We work longer days with more responsibility and less job security.

Many people are searching for greater integrity and sense of balance. This scenario challenges us to re-examine our commitments to maintain a sense of balance. And yet, few know how to take on that challenge.

As recently as the mid-'80s, the boundaries between work and home were more clearly defined. Most Americans worked an eight-hour day. In 1986, I worked at a commercial bank. Like most companies at the time, we relied on the U.S. Postal Service for our correspondence. We had a typing pool. Documents were produced only as fast as the pool could deliver. Writing was a much more methodical process. Our work required more time to accomplish. It was not nearly as portable. When we left the office, we left the work. We were not *virtually* connected by technology – cell phones, pagers, or e-mail. After work, we could more completely relax with family or friends, pursue our hobbies – ground ourselves.

Today, our aspiration to affluence is like the alien in *Body Snatchers*. Our vitality is sucked away every time we justify not living our true lives. We are chronically fatigued because we feel victimized by our commitments, and we don't know what to do about it.

However, we cannot blame technology for our hectic pace and over-committed schedules. Technology has simply made it easier to push ourselves, farther, faster. We are energetic beings, encoded with an instinct for self-preservation. Today, that self-preservation must include developing a deeper awareness and understanding of what it takes to live joyously in such a complex world. And technology can help us do it. Through the electronic transfer of information, the sharing of ideas and ideals is easier than ever before. Satellite technology has made it possible for us to experience life – real time anywhere in the world. Technology is helping science build a bridge to the unseen as physicians and physicists alike are able to observe, measure, and analyze the energy of not only our world, but our universe.

We cannot separate the technology from humanity. Technology now has a life of its own. As such, we must see how the act of self-preservation is no longer limited to members of the plant and animal kingdoms. I believe all energetic systems evolve and therefore act to self-preserve. We have developed a technological consciousness that demands and manifests its own change via human catalysts.

Organizations are also energetic systems with a life of their own. As with the human body, the corporate body seeks to heal itself after injury. Just think about what happens when a person is fired or quits; like a trauma to the body, the company works around the damage until a replacement is found and the wound is healed.

Reorganizations and restructurings are like going on a diet or adding exercise to your schedule. The idea is to improve the health and, hopefully, the longevity of the company.

Like the human body, the organization is self-perpetuating and always working. The job is never complete. Whether you're an at-home parent, a car mechanic, or a bank vice-president, there's always more work to do – the principle of self-preservation demands constant maintenance.

While technology continues to manifest change exponentially, we can shift it into its proper role in our lives. We can acknowledge our participation and our position and then choose to find the balance in our lives.

WHY DO WE WORK SO HARD?

The human spirit has an inherent desire to serve. What we're attempting to do when we unhappily commit to working 50, 60, or more hours per week is to contribute while simultaneously satisfying our inherent need to feel secure. Unfortunately, our inspiration is often the fear of lack. We maintain the status quo because we're afraid of what will happen if we don't. However, an ongoing commitment of body, mind, and spirit to negatively inspired action can lead to breakdowns that even substantial financial reward cannot prevent.

The work you do should be an extension of who you are. What you do should enrich your life by allowing you to express yourself fully. Otherwise, it's like choosing a diet made up solely of cotton candy. It's a superficial web of delight, spun in bright hues to tickle the eye and dance on the tongue, and yet, lacks any nutritional value. Even if you try to fill up on it, it will not sustain you. You need other nutrients.

We live in the most affluent country in the world with access to any resource imaginable. Yet, we continue to be plagued emotionally, physically and spiritually. Diseases like diabetes, heart disease, and high blood pressure, are in many cases, lifestyle diseases. They should be manageable; however, their incidence is on the rise. The news is filled with stories of violence and tragedy committed not only amongst strangers, but by one neighbor against another, or husband against wife, or employee against employer. Dissatisfaction with the lack of balance in our lives is peaking. People are starved for relief.

I QUIT

Approximately 51 percent of Americans prefer more free time, even if it means less income[1].

So, if we want it, why don't we have it? I believe we have lost our sense of alignment– clarity of focus, intention and commitment. We do not regularly discern what we truly want. Or, if we know what we want, we often lack the trust or faith in ourselves to go after it. Making more money tends to stimulate our fears of not having it, which makes us more attached to making money. It's a vicious cycle.

We would love to isolate the cause of our discomfort from the effect. We want to separate the risk of taking action from living the life we want. However, they are inseparable. We want to blame and complain but, as Dan Millman put it in *The Laws of Spirit*, "we have no friends or enemies, just teachers." We must learn to look for the broad lessons, to search for our truths and to be responsible for creating the life we want to live.

Lacey was working long hours as vice-president of operations. Little engaged her about the work, the place or the people. As she would say, she had not been raised to be "airy-fairy," and yet, nothing felt right. Lacey had been highly intuitive all of her life, but couldn't find a satisfying outlet for sharing her talents of insight and inspiration. A difficult personal relationship further discouraged her from looking closely at herself and the life that she wanted–it was too painful. She withdrew from nearly all of her personal relationships and focused solely on work. At one point Lacey developed a tumor in her right leg. She ignored it and continued to limit the expression of herself to her work. She did not acknowledge how bad it was getting for her on any level, emotionally, physically, spiritually, or intellectually. Lacey recalls how often she would think about her work and say, "I can't stand this."

And then, one day she literally couldn't stand. Her body broke down in response to the emotional, intellectual, and physical challenges she was enduring. The tumor had become very large and life-threatening. It required surgery and an eight-week recovery, during which time she was forced to look at the state of her life. She realized she had been hiding out from the life she wanted for the last 20 years. She had to choose whether to return to a life that lacked "aliveness" or take a different path. She admitted that she did not want to go back to her job and was happy to find out that her company could not afford to pay her anymore.

Recuperating and unemployed, she took a few classes that helped her look closely at her life and introduced her to practical ways she could use her intuition and interpersonal skills. Lacey is now honoring her truth, paying close attention to, and trusting her self-guidance. She is now more fully expressing herself by designing Web pages, training in Reiki – a form of energetic healing – channeling, and working with people to help them get in touch with their inner voice.

What if I told you that you could do work that brings you joy and be successful at it? What if you could experience the life you dream of? It can be done. You must start with your truth.

I QUIT

The bridge between truth and the life you want to live is trust in one's self. It requires a change in perspective, a willingness to discover your truths, to honor them, and to trust in them. You must release any attachment you have to the value of anyone else's opinion of your life over your own.

HOW DO WE FIX IT?

We would love a quick, clear-cut fix to the work/life balance challenge. We are trained to immediately move into *doing something,* to fix what *seems* to be broken. But a quick fix doesn't exist. There are quick answers which may feel like fixes, but without reflection they may end up as diversions. A fix based on truth and integrity requires a time-out reflection. Circumstances are not our enemy; in fact, they are our opportunities to choose, change, and grow. We must acknowledge that we are not simply acted upon by invisible forces, or visible forces like friends, family, our jobs, churches, or the government. Whether we want to recognize it or not, we are actively engaged in this thing called life. Whether we are conscious of it, or not, we are constantly co-creating. We *are* responsible for the choices we make, the actions we take, and the ones we don't take.

All action requires some level of personal commitment and direction. Successful action requires focus, intention, and commitment. Sometimes this takes the form of ambition and passion. If you use these traits fully, you are likely to succeed. If the *source* for your inspiration, however, is negative – revenge, for instance – or if it is not authentically your own, there will eventually be dissatisfaction, discomfort, pain, or failure. The greatest accomplishments require starting from the purest source – your own voice. Understand that no one will simply hand you a peaceful, joyous life, but that you can co-create it along with the limitless power of the universe.

To aspire is a uniquely human trait. Strong aspirations to serve have led many people on to accomplishments. A life fueled with an intention to serve can lead to unparalleled satisfaction. However, you must know what you truly want, and commit yourself to accomplishing it. When I use the term service, I don't mean to be servile. I mean to enrich your life and another's with the actions you take. Virtually everything we do can be done with this intention.

I know that my imagination and my free will/choice are the most powerful tools I possess. I know that all things great and small are delivered through the doorway of my imagination. I know that I always have the power of my perspective. I can either look for the lesson in every encounter, or I can simply cast myself to the wind and watch my life blow away. I understand that in every experience, especially the negative ones, if I don't look for the lesson, I have chosen to go sailing without a captain.

One of the most powerful ways I've found for people to find their way to personal peace starts with the work they do. It's not only the task, but also the approach and embodiment of the task. Is it done with honesty? Integrity? Is it serving you? Our work is an extension of who we are.

The possibility exists for every person to know peace by recognizing and embracing their own values and dreams. When you are satisfied with your life, feeling no lack, you lose any resentment toward others for what they seem to have, or could be seen as keeping from you. There is no reason for antagonism between two people when each is fulfilled in themselves.

When most of us talk about how we spend our time daily, we're talking about the work we do. This book is designed to help you find the work you love by clarifying the vision of your life. Out of this vision will fall the tasks, interactions, and activities that bring you the greatest satisfaction. From there you can look for a context in which to deploy them.

If we can be truthful with ourselves about what makes us happy. If we can be courageous and respect our dreams instead of letting them collect dust in the attics of our hearts; if we can be responsible and do something to move us toward integrating those dreams into our lives, then will we find greater peace and satisfaction.

SECTION TWO

Choosing work that aligns with your soul

WHAT DOES IT REQUIRE?

"What is my job on the planet? Is one question we might do well to ask ourselves over and over again. Otherwise, we may wind up doing somebody else's job and not even know it. And what's more, that somebody might be a figment of our own imagination and maybe a prisoner of it as well."

> Jon Kabat-Zinn
> *Wherever You go, There You Are:*[2]
> *Mindfullness Meditation in Everyday Life*

Choosing work that brings you joy requires knowing who you are, what you want, and not waiting for permission to go after it. It does not arrive based on entitlement or simple expectation. When you choose work that aligns with your soul, you no longer spend your time judging others or yourself with thoughts of right or wrong. When you choose joy, you stop ignoring the discomfort in your life and face it head on. You choose three principles to live by: truth, trust, and responsibility.

You must respect yourself enough to be truthful about who you are and then act responsibly to move forward regardless of what anyone else might say. Statements like, "I wish I could," or "I had no choice" will become obsolete as you come to better understand the power of choice. Choosing work that brings you joy means searching for peace by living with loving intentions. It means finding your gift, your passion, and then *serving* the greater good by sharing it.

It's imperative that you know what you do well, what brings you joy or pain. Satisfaction is a product of authentic expression. Joy is the pinnacle of authentic expression. When you live authentically,

Karyn Pettigrew

you don't have the need for fatalistic competition. The zero-sum game will not exist because you'll understand that in life, for you to win, I don't have to lose.

So long as we look outside of ourselves for validation of our worth, we are risking great disappointment and disillusionment. Who are you if you lose your money, possessions, even your family? Do you know? Can you define yourself outside of the things you have? Or what you do? When you try to do this, is it difficult? This book will help you discern your own voice amongst the myriad other voices we are constantly exposed to.

I QUIT

THE JOY/PAIN LIST

Make a list of those activities, people, and experiences that bring you joy or pain, where pain can be any form of discomfort, not necessarily physical pain. Be thoughtful; this list is for your own clarity.

JOY	PAIN

Karyn Pettigrew

The joy/pain list is a starting point for your change. Those things that bring you pain must be released. Begin working on ways that you can responsibly separate yourself from the people and activities that are painful.

The things that bring you joy are the things that must be integrated more completely into your life. This is the fertile source material for work that will align with your soul.

HOW DO YOU DEFINE YOURSELF?

Take a few minutes and define yourself. Use any language or description that you feel comfortable with.

_____

_____

_____

_____

_____

_____

_____

_____

_____

_____

_____

_____

_____

_____

_____

_____

_____

_____

_____

_____

_____

Many people define themselves in relation to another person. "Hi, I'm John's wife," or "Margaret's daughter," or "I work for Ken." Others start with a label that expresses the kind of daily work activity they engage in: "I work at Big Bank" or "I'm in retail at Lookin' Good Clothes." This is completely understandable since we put so very much of ourselves into the work we do. However, defining ourselves by the tasks we do is one-dimensional. It fails to adequately capture all of who we are. That one-dimensional view of our "self" is the source of pain for many people today. We have placed limitations on our self-expression and assigned value to our lives based on the job title we hold. To add to it, the more money we make, the more likely we are to identify with our jobs. An over-identification of "what we do," as "who we are," eventually settles in our bones to the point where we begin to believe and see ourselves as the job, when the job should be seen as a context for expressing who we are.

An over-identification with the job is what leads to so much emotional damage when we're downsized, right-sized, criticized, or skipped-over for promotion. We take it personally because we've forgotten that the job (where we work) is only one context, of many, where we express who we are. When we move to any new job, the context changes, but our talents and gifts go with us. *Who we are* is portable. Who we are is defined in the way we do our job, by the choices we make, and the intention behind those choices, not by the job title. We have a tendency to forget that we are so much more than the tasks we do. Again, this is understandable since we are usually evaluated by our tasks; yet, this is exactly the reason we must become reacquainted with ourselves. Regardless of the challenge or fear, we must be able to find our way to our truth in the moment. Life is dynamic; what was truth for us 10 years ago, may not be so today.

xternal context is never relevant to your ability to live your
... .. , ou truly are. In every instance we have the opportunity to
express ourselves authentically – in a bank, on the bus, or at the
job. When you do, regardless of the challenge, you will find
peace.

At 39, shortly after quitting her job to become a full-time mom,
Becky began feeling that something was missing, but she wasn't
sure what it was. She only knew that change was coming. And it
did. Shortly thereafter, her husband left her.

Becky found a lucrative job in medical sales, but was unhappy.
She would find herself shopping instead of on her sales calls.
When she was on her sales calls, she often found the doctors and
nurses looking to her for insight and motivation as opposed to the
products she had to sell. Her product line was feeding tubes, but
instead of selling them for the patients, she found herself feeding
the souls of the doctor's nurses.

Eventually, Becky connected the dots in her own history. In
college, she had majored in public speaking and communications.
Her life experience had provided her with the anecdotal evidence
that people were drawn to her for advice and inspiration. What
she recognized and accepted is that "who she was" included
being a motivational force for positive change.   She was ready to
claim that as her own.

Becky acknowledges the power of facing her own truth and
trusting that the path to her heart's desire would open when she
was willing to face her truths. After this breakthrough, she met a
man who became her husband. He married a fuller expression of
Becky, one who is living her truths daily. Becky's new husband
provided the financial stability that allowed her to quit her job. For
the past five years she has been doing motivational public
speaking and intuitive life-coaching.

One of the things that Becky's story illustrates is the concept of our "life tool kit."

Inside our tool kit is the collection of our life's experiences. All of it—life's triumphs and tragedies—is meant to serve us, to help create the platform on which we stand and from which we direct our lives. If we examine these experiences closely, we can begin to connect the dots. We can tie together actions and activities that help to show us who we really are. In Becky's case she was finally able to see that her gifts included public speaking, and communicating messages of hope. Everyone has a tool kit that can be an enormous resource filled with information and inspiration, if we choose to look inside.

Take a look at the list of descriptors on the next page. The words are rich but unfortunately underused. Use this list to begin to flush out a new description of yourself. Look back over the years for trends in your actions, activities, and interests. What are the consistencies? Don't judge! Some of the terms may have negative connotations, but be honest if it helps to describe who you are today.

LIST OF DESCRIPTORS

Addict (includes TV, work, sports, etc)	**Healer**
Advocate	**Jokester**
Angel	**Leader**
Artist	**Lover**
Athlete	**Martyr**
Avenger	**Mediator**
Bully	**Mentor**
Counselor	**Mother**
Engineer	**Pioneer**
Father	**Rescuer**
Friend	**Servant**
Grouch	**Student**
Hero/Heroine	**Visionary**

There are no "right" or "wrong" descriptors. However, you'll probably notice that I'm not using typical titles like doctor, lawyer, banker. These labels tend to be one-dimensional. The descriptor list is designed to help expand our vocabulary as we expand our understanding of who we are and what we want in our lives. Feel free to use any additional language that describes who you are today. In the space provided below, write a revised description of who you are today and compare it with the description of yourself you wrote on page 30.

advocate, nurturer, willful, temperamental, patient, counselor,

I QUIT

MY STORY – DISCOVERING A DEFINITION OF MYSELF

In 1996 I was working as Deputy Director of Marketing at the Illinois state lottery. I had been with the agency for three years and was beginning to feel like I wanted a change. The only promotion open to me was agency director, a Governor-appointed position. For many reasons, I could see how unlikely that was.

So, one day I asked myself, "If I could do work at anything I wanted to tomorrow, what would that be?" I couldn't answer the question. I drew a complete blank. For the first time in my life, I didn't have a plan. For as long as I could remember, I had always had a plan. In high school I knew that my next step was college. At Wellesley I knew that I wanted to be in business and was accepted to Harvard Business School. Following business school, I wanted to work in brand management so I went to work for Quaker Oats.

There had always been clear, logical, conventional next steps. Except now, for the first time, I was unable to see where I was going, or to really identify what was important to me. This was the beginning of my self-investigation. I was determined to discover what was important to me. I was confident in my skills as a marketer and general manager, and yet I was feeling antsy and ready for something different. I wanted to work for an organization where my experience and talents could really lead it forward.

I started the introspective process by asking myself how I wanted to use my talents. My first answer was – in the not-for-profit sector. For some reason, that just didn't feel right. I had been sitting on the board of directors for two not-for-profit organizations and while I loved working with them, I knew I wanted something

Karyn Pettigrew

else. Shortly after I asked myself that question, my former boss at the lottery approached me about joining her team at the local natural-gas utility. They were preparing for deregulation of the industry and wanted to reposition the brand. It sounded like an interesting challenge. I would take my brand and marketing experience to an organization on the verge of significant change. I had also really enjoyed working with my former boss. She had been a friend and a mentor. I knew that we made a good team, so I signed on. Even as I was fully committed to doing a great job, the question of what I truly wanted never left me.

As I thought about what I wanted to do, I discovered I was fascinated with the possibility of working at what we love. I wanted to know what motivated people to do things that seem to go against conventional thought, or to lead them outside of what they were trained to do. What fueled that person in the face of adversity? There had been some mass media coverage on the subject: *Passion in our work.* Even Oprah was doing features on it. I became obsessed with how people make decisions about the work they do, what makes us happy, and how that contributes to our health. I had one particularly fun question to ask people at parties which was, "if they could wave a magic wand and immediately work at anything they wanted, what would it be?" Without exception, I would get answers that, at the core, reflected a commitment to service and a connection with others. Answers that came straight from the heart:

- The art director of my ad agency wanted to paint and do something with children in art.
- The public relations manager at my company wanted to work with children in the public schools.
- A co-worker wanted to do transpersonal psychology.

I QUIT

- A woman in a group that I facilitate wanted to establish a special agency network to help families in need of nursing or hospice care.
- A co-worker wanted to study law and help at-risk women and children.
- A friend wanted to open a coffee café in an area that had nothing like it.

The answers I received go on and on like these. The more I contemplated my little experiment, the deeper I dug into the meaning of my existence. I began studying metaphysics and holistic healing. I read and read and read. I attended lectures and workshops. I met amazing people who had skills that I never imagined.

One such person was Sonia Choquette. She is an intuitive, an author, a spiritual teacher and is now my friend. She recommended a particular workshop that would help me break through the emotional, intellectual, and spiritual barriers that were keeping me from fully experiencing my life. This workshop, called the Hoffman Quadrinity Process, is a 10-day residency program offered world-wide. It was a profound experience.

Deeply into the course I realized that I really wanted to work in the area of personal empowerment and healing. I began to envision a new way of looking at what it means to be healthy. I began to see a healing continuum that includes complementary therapies such as chiropractic medicine, acupuncture, auyervedic, and massage therapy, integrated with allopathic or western medicine. I saw and began to design a holistic center where people would have access to therapists, workshops and healing meditation. It would be an urban oasis for physical, spiritual, and emotional healing. Little did I know at the time, that it was just the beginning of living my truth.

SECTION THREE

Where to begin?

KNOW HOW YOU SEE THINGS

The work that we do should provide financial support as a by-product of sharing the best part of ourselves. Work that aligns with our soul, journeys directly out of the vision we hold for ourselves. When we see the contribution that our work makes and know that it comes from the vision we create for ourselves, we can feel sated by it.

Choosing work that aligns with your soul is ultimately about you and how you see things. Are you living from a perspective of possibilities or from a perspective of lack? Guided by a perspective of possibilities and the principles of truth, trust, and responsibility, you will be led to a true vision of the life you want to live.

KNOW YOUR TRUTH

"Truth is the only thing that stands between broken hearts and wholeness"

Sarah Ban Breathnach
Something More[3]

The truth sits patiently in our hearts. Only you know when you are being or have been completely truthful. There is a difference between something that is intellectually true and a truth from your "knowing heart." An intellectual true-ism is often rationalized. You arrive at it. It is a logical conclusion. And it generally takes more time to materialize. Your knowing heart provides truths instantaneously. For example, it is true that I went to the dinner party. The truth is that I didn't want to go. The truth digs deeper. It moves beyond the facts to the intent and feelings behind the facts.

You definitely need your intellect to manifest things in your life, but the truth about what you want to manifest comes from your heart, not your head. Your intellect is the conduit for physical manifestation, but it's also the source of the ego, and the ego is interested only in safety and survival. Generally, your ego will be adverse to risks that will move it beyond what it knows and is comfortable with. This applies to everyone, even those who you might consider a natural risk taker.

For instance, a woman who had been trading commodities for five years was used to the ups and downs of the market. Turning on a dime and making split decisions was something that came easily when the subject was pork-bellies. However, she was not so "risk-tolerant" at the thought of returning to business school. She hesitated because her trading paid the bills. It was predictable, safe.

When I refer to a knowing heart, what I'm talking about is being able to discern a knowing that comes straight to you from yourself as source, versus a thought that has been intellectualized, amended, or watered down by negative beliefs or other people's comments. A heart-led decision will always be authentic – your purest, cleanest decision. It will leave you with the greatest peace although it may not feel that way at first. In your heart you'll know it's right. That doesn't mean that your decision will be easy to execute or easy for others to accept.

The knowing heart that I speak of should not be confused with romantic emotionalism. I'm not talking about being emotionally moved to a certain decision, by things like guilt, lust, infatuation, or the need to rescue. I'm talking about a gut-check and an honesty that only you and the universe may ever be able to confirm. We may, through our intellect attempt to suppress this truth, shelve it, or rationalize it out of existence. But your knowing heart will not lie. We must learn how to see our truths, trust ourselves enough to honor that truth and then act responsibly.

Acting on our truth is not a zero-sum practice. It's about learning to see from the perspective of possibilities rather than the perspective of lack where lack is the perception that something is missing—I am without, or will be without. However, in order for me to have, you don't have to go without. Abundance has no favorites, people do. The possibilities are endless if you choose to be creative.

No one loses. You may wonder how I can say this. In the moment you may experience loss, but that perception can be released if you choose to let it go. The first thing is to change perspective regarding what it means to *not get* what you think you want and therefore lose. Perhaps not getting what you want or think you want is a way of showing you alternatives. We may very well be without something we want, or lacking, but that does not necessitate that we live in a state of lack. When we are in a state of lack, a state of doubting our abilities, we fail to see the greater possibilities, and therefore remain unable to manifest something better.

Pick an instance where you didn't get something that you wanted. If you honestly and carefully review everything in the chain of events in support of that desire, I believe you will find a weak link. An inability to pursue your goal can only come from one place – you. Perhaps in your case:

- you didn't really want it
- you doubted your ability to get it
- you secretly, deeply, wanted something else.
- you needed to attend to something else first
- you defined the desired outcome too narrowly and limited its' creative development or,
- you ended up with something better

Knowing and following your truth is the first critical element in choosing work that aligns with your soul. It does not require someone else, or replacing something else for you to gain personal peace. To create in the physical world, we must first maintain a perspective of possibilities, we must focus on our vision, believe in it, commit our resources to it, and then allow the universe to collaborate with us.

I QUIT

COMPOSTING REGRETS

No experience is ever wasted. Every experience offers valuable lessons for our life tool kit. The experiences we classify as good will seem obvious in their benefits. However, those experiences which are difficult or painful rarely seem to hold value. Yet, they do. We must dig in and look for the lessons in adversity.

One really good exercise to help liberate the lessons buried within our challenges is to compost our regrets. When we harbor regrets, we are also denying our truth. A regret is an acknowledgement that, sometime in the past, we did not, or were unable to act on our truth. Unreconciled regrets are another source of "dead weight." Unrealized aspirations hang around turning our creative energy into waste. The chart provided below is designed to help you compost your regrets. Make a list of everything you regret. When you are finished, go back to each item and decide what you choose to do with it. You have the choice to:

1) Release it, meaning forgive yourself for not following your heart, or feeling guilty about something you could not control. Or,

2) Recycle it, meaning outline action that will incorporate that regret into the vision you are creating for your life.

Upon closer review, the things that you want to recycle will provide insight into who you are by highlighting aspects that have been neglected. The first three items on the list are provided as examples.

Karyn Pettigrew

COMPOSTING REGRETS WORKSHEET

#	List your regret	Your Choice Release	Complete	Action you will take to complete
Ex. A	Not studying abroad in college		X	Plan annual trip to a place that I've always wanted to go.
Ex. B	Not being at my mother-in-law's bedside at her death.		X	Write a letter to her now, explaining how I felt then and now.
Ex. C	Breaking up with college boyfriend through non-action.	X		
1				
2				
3				
4				

I QUIT

One of my friends and students, Barbara had just left her retail management job of 16 years. She had been happy at the job, but a recent acquisition by a larger retailer had led to significant changes in management policy. The new policies didn't allow for the kind of creative environment she wanted. She found herself working longer and harder with less flexibility. After the September 11 World Trade Center tragedy, she had even been given some security-type duties. Eventually, she found a new job at another retailer but a non-compete clause in her agreement with her former company, required a one-month cooling-off period. She was looking forward to the "forced vacation." It would provide an opportunity to do some of the things that she hadn't had time to do, like remodeling work around the house, spending more time with her husband, and simply relaxing. She was very excited about having the time to get to some of her interests.

On her second day home, Barbara's husband was trying to figure out what he could change in his schedule that would enable him to take his sister, who didn't drive, to the doctor. Since Barbara was home, she offered to take her sister-in-law. She figured that she would have plenty of time that afternoon to prepare for class she was registered for that evening. However, after the doctor, her sister-in-law asked if they could pick up a few things from the supermarket. Barbara wanted to say no, she really needed the time to prepare for the workshop, but she said yes. In the end, she ran out of time and was unable to prepare for the class.

Barbara's afternoon was not as she had hoped because she sacrificed the time she needed to prepare. As a result, she felt some resentment and disappointment. We've all been in situations like that of Barbara's where we put something that was important

Karyn Pettigrew

to us aside for someone or something else. Service to others is one of the keys to universal alignment; however, we must recognize that a commitment made to ourselves is just as valid as one we make to someone else.

This is a co-creative universe and there are ways to serve others without constantly sacrificing ourselves. A truthful, self-loving, and responsible solution might have been for Barbara to let her know that she really wanted to prepare for a class that evening and if they could go to the supermarket the next day. If her sister-in-law needed something right away, Barbara might have had it at her own home, or perhaps her husband could have picked it up. In all likelihood, her sister-in-law would have understood and been willing to co-create a solution for both of them.

Generally, our friends and family will want to work with us on solutions. It's amazing to me how responsive people have been when I speak the truth from my heart with a willingness to co-create a solution. If you find yourself compromising what's important to you, don't chastise yourself, just realize what's happening and try to find a win-win solution. If you experience many of these "little" self-denials, take a closer look at your motivation for doing it. What do you want in return? Something concrete? Something emotional? Think back; did you get what you wanted? Were you satisfied? Asking yourself these questions will help to redirect your actions to what you really want.

TRUST YOURSELF

"One cannot give to a person that which he already possesses"
Toussaint L'Ouverture
Proclamation, March 1, 1802

Trust is such an empowering concept, and yet we constantly miss opportunities to embrace it. Think about the number of times you've said, "I knew that would happen" or "I should have done it the way I wanted to in the first place." Trusting yourself means following your hunches. It means honoring your innate wisdom and the miracles that you can, and do, create for yourself. Trust means to have a love of yourself that will allow you to do what's right for you – irrespective of what others think you should do. You may not regularly entertain thoughts about what you'd *like* to do, but you probably think a lot about what you *need* to do. Thinking about what you'd like to do may seem self-indulgent, frivolous, or touchy-feely, and you may have strong beliefs about your responsibility to others before yourself. Whatever your opinions, I'm asking you to grant yourself the same grace you extend to others in your life. No one can give you trust in yourself. You must believe in yourself.

Doing what is right for you first, and then striving to live selflessly, may seem to rub against all we are taught about helping others. But it is

- knowing who you are;
- knowing what you need;
- knowing what brings you joy;

that will allow you to experience a satisfying fullness of spirit and in turn be even more present, loving, and helpful to others.

For most of her life, Pamela had taken the safe route. She had followed her parents' directions and done what was prudent. After college she went to business school and received her MBA. In the early '90's, MBAs were in great demand. Pamela knew that having the degree would provide her an entree into any number of possible careers. Pamela's last position was in health-care marketing. She didn't know why, but the job was not giving her the excitement and fulfillment she was looking for.

Pamela began to explore an old area of interest–entertainment. She took a writing course and began a screen play. She also began thinking about how she could get into the entertainment industry. Since there were rumors of a possible takeover of her company, the timing was perfect for her contemplated change.As she talked to friends and family about her desire to work in entertainment, she was met with a lot of well-meaning opposition. "Are you sure?" "You're so good at your job. You could really go places." "Do you know how hard it is to get into entertainment?" Her family could not comprehend her decision.

Pamela realized she was at a crossroad. She knew she had to listen to her own voice and choose to act on her own guidance. While she recognized her family and friends had her best interest at heart, she had to put their admonitions aside.

I QUIT

When she focused on what she wanted and committed herself fully, she received two job interviews in entertainment marketing. Neither position was on the same level as her health-care job, but getting in the door was her first goal. She was confident in her ability to perform once she was inside. As Pamela puts it, her greatest lesson was, "not to be afraid to step back in order to step forward." In listening to her own voice, Pamela could see the greater opportunity.

For Pamela, the field of entertainment is her opportunity to institute positive change in the world as well as in herself. It is through the entertainment industry that she will serve and share her talents. She is working on a screenplay and has begun writing a self-enhancement activity workbook targeted at urban youth. Her goal is to project positive images in urban communities using entertainment as a vehicle for communication.

When you act selflessly, you interact with people, not because of what you expect them to give you in return, but because you want to—purely and simply.

Shifting your focus from, "how I rank versus you," or from a perspective of lack, you open up to an entirely new level of consciousness—toward greater selflessness.

Take caution! Doing what is right for you is not permission to go on a narcissistic binge irresponsibly leaving friends and family in a mangled heap. When you do what is right for you it must be done responsibly and without intention to harm another.

Trusting yourself means being courageous enough to search beneath your patterned response, or behavior, to find your truth. It means that you will acknowledge your truth now instead of tucking it away neatly behind *sometime tomorrow*. It means believing that your thoughts, dreams, and desires have value.

Sometimes we are wounded physically or emotionally, and in order to protect ourselves we contract. Out of fear we pull back our emotions, vigor, and willingness to take a risk. When we allow the fear created by these wounds to remain unexamined, we tend to imagine the worst. But if we examine our fear, literally pull it out of the ether and into the physical world by speaking of it or writing it down – somehow it loses potency. By acknowledging it, you can begin to work on it.

Write down your fears on the following lines. Write down the big and little things that bring you pause. You don't have to do anything with this list right now. Writing them down is simply a conscious acknowledgement of what haunts you. Trust yourself to see these fears in the light so that when you're ready, you can put your total resources to work on erasing them.

FEAR LIST

_____

_____

_____

_____

_____

_____

_____

_____

_____

_____

_____

_____

_____

Every time you deny your own wisdom by doing what others want you to do and not listening to your own inner-voice, you hand over your power. Every time we say yes when we want to say no, we're turning our backs on our own truth and trusting someone else's desires for us above our own. In doing so, another little piece of us fades into the background. Trust asks if you can live with your decisions even if no one else supports them. It asks if you can do what you need to for your own fulfillment. Can you go on despite the possible rejection because you know it's the right thing to do? Can you ask for help when you need it? Choosing to live your life in alignment requires that you trust yourself – your decisions, your intuition, your needs and desires – so that they will lead you to what will benefit you most.

Karyn Pettigrew

BE RESPONSIBLE

"You will only need to trust yourself to make responsible choices."

don Miguel Ruiz
The Four Agreements

We must be responsible for our own lives. We must write our own stories. If anyone else is holding your pen, you will never write a true word. We can no longer expect others to take care of us, or to decide for us. Nor can we wait for things to happen to us. When we experience discomfort we must take heed of the signals and review our lives for what is out of alignment.

No one can know what you need and want better than you. No one can know what you feel as clearly as you do. No one can save you, but you. All anyone outside of you can do is act as a catalyst for your change. Doctors don't heal you; they serve as catalysts for your healing. You heal you! By your attitude and commitment to a treatment plan. Your mind, body and spirit must be in alignment for the most complete recovery; if they are not, the problem is likely to return or manifest as something else.

You may say, well, if that's true, what about babies who become ill? Are they healing themselves? I say yes, with guidance and caring by adults. All illnesses are created by imbalances. Although, the sources—nutritional, chemical, environmental, emotional—may vary, babies can be exposed to any and all of them. To me, the source is less relevant than the patient's general disposition toward healing. Children's natural disposition is toward the management of their basic needs – food, warmth, and love. They generally maintain an openness that works with the healer to restore balance.

Being responsible requires that you move yourself toward your dreams. You create opportunities by heightening your awareness and doing all that you can to position yourself to intercept information that will help you.

Mona and her husband had been invited to invest in the production of a film. Their first reaction was, 'No way! We don't know the first thing about movie-making." They couldn't tell a good risk from a bad one, so they initially declined the offer. But their friend was not easily dissuaded and explained more about how the production process worked. The couple reconsidered and decided to invest. The project went on to deliver a reasonable return.

Investing in the movie reminded Mona of one of her life's passions–the theater and acting. Growing up, Mona had always been involved in theater. But that world had taken a back seat to her career in radio where she is a top executive at the number one station in her market. Despite her powerful career, her soul was stirred.

Following the decision to invest in the film, Mona attended a film-and-acting boot camp in Florida. She went partly because she and her husband felt they needed greater familiarity with the industry and partly because she was being called back to her truth. After returning from the boot camp Mona began making moves to learn even more about the film business. One phone call led to another which led to another, until she found herself with possible entrees to film financing, production, screen-writing, and acting. With Phil, one of those contacts, she had been particularly focused and trusting of the inner voice that told her to remain committed.

To her dismay, they would schedule a meeting and he would cancel. After several months, Mona called Phil and suggested that perhaps they should stop trying to get together. The timing did not seem to support connecting, and she knew that he was a very busy man. Phil refused to let it go and picked a day he would be in her city. On the day of the meeting, Mona got stuck in an important regional sales meeting. She knew it was going to run over and cause her to miss her meeting with Phil. In that moment she chose to be responsible to her dreams. She took a leap of faith and left the sales meeting. She had worked so hard to create the opportunity with Phil that she felt compelled to join him. She put her marketing manager in charge of the rest of the sales meeting and never looked back.

Mona had a good meeting with Phil that offered interesting possibilities. Just before she left, Phil's next appointment arrived. When she was introduced to the gentleman, he was surprised to find that she worked at a radio station he knew well. He mentioned that years ago, he had really enjoyed working with another executive at the station. That executive turned out to be Mona's husband! The three of them immediately bonded. As a result, interesting projects continue to be presented to Mona and her husband.

The real story here is not Mona's decision to take a risk, or even the role of her tool kit – the series of experiences that prepares and directs us toward our authenticity. The real story is the *power of responsibility*. Mona took responsibility for her dreams and it paid off.

I QUIT

MY STORY OF TRUTH, TRUST AND RESPONSIBILITY

My last 15 months at the natural gas utility had been intense. We had three corporate crises in a row. My area of the company was responsible for corporate marketing and communications. We used to joke that a crisis-management specialist could have rounded out their career in that year.

In the fall of 2000 we launched a mercury contamination investigation that involved our city-wide and north suburban territories; in that winter the cost of natural gas spiked almost 300 percent, and in the spring of 2001 we suffered the first union strike in 35 years. It was a stressful year, but the company performed well. Surprisingly, it wasn't the series of crises that triggered my signal to leave; it was what followed.

In the fall of 2001, my boss approached me about a promotion. By then, I was several years into my spiritual studies. I had even been working on designing a wellness center. A promotion would mean more responsibility, although presumably not at the same intensity level as the previous year. As I thought about the possible role that lay before me, I realized I would have to significantly reduce my spiritual studies in order to focus on a new position. I knew I couldn't spread myself any thinner. On top of my 50-60-hour- per-week job I had two young children and a household to manage.

I was at a crossroad in my life. I was being presented with an opportunity to step up in the organization, but to me that signaled more work. Despite the up-front intention of getting back to normal in the organization, my experience reminded me that every previous promotion had come with an increased time commitment.

Karyn Pettigrew

I had much to consider. First, I was well-compensated, and as my husband is self-employed, I carried our whole family on my health-care plan. Fears about money, health care insurance, and my husband's uncertainty about the holistic arena, were pervasive.

For two months I debated the options with myself and God. I meditated, I prayed, I analyzed the possible outcomes. Leaving my current job to pursue what I could not clearly define, or guarantee would be economically viable, was frightening. I thought about what it would mean to leave people I liked and a terrific career opportunity. I knew that a lot of work was being put into corporate restructuring. I also knew that I could have a place on the senior team. However, it was hard for me to consider accepting a new position in good faith, knowing that I had such strong feelings about doing more work in holistic health.

My signals came in the form of a fairly dramatic weight loss, moodiness at home, and a few uncharacteristically "off-performances" at work. Enough of me was at odds that a few weeks before Christmas my boss sat me down and asked what was up. I didn't tell her everything I was feeling because, while we had developed a wonderful relationship over the eight years that we worked together, she was still my boss and I didn't want to color her perception of me if I decided to stay. We agreed that over Christmas I would think carefully about what I wanted.

My husband and I went back and forth over the household budget. One minute we could see the light, and the next we were questioning the feasibility of it all. Part of our challenge was that he wasn't into the metaphysical, holistic thing. Quite frankly, there were times when he thought that I had lost it, with all my books, discussions, and classes. Thankfully, we kept hammering

I QUIT

away at how we could make my exit work. We finally figured out that we could cut expenses, he could draw a little more from the business, and I could consult to fill in the gaps.

Once we had the budget worked out, I was left to think about how I, the woman who had spent all her adult life accumulating credentials to demonstrate her legitimacy in the business world, had ended up with one foot out of the door with not one appropriate credential in a new field. I spent more time in meditation, prayer, and finally an acknowledgement of the subtle, supportive hints that the Universe had sent me in the form of coincidences, chance encounters, and simple resonances.

I also reminded myself that I still had great credentials and solid relationships that could get me back into the corporate world if I needed to. More than anything else, it just felt right. It may have looked crazy, but I knew it was right. I can't explain why I felt supported, but I did. This knowing, combined with my stockpile of credentials, led to my leap of faith. I decided to leave the company and go for my dream. I took my boss to breakfast as soon as she returned from the Christmas holiday. She was saddened, but supportive, with a deep appreciation that I was doing what was right for me. We planned to get things in line by restructuring the department and hiring my replacement before making a general announcement. But as things usually happen in organizations, the grapevine was infallible. A leak forced us to announce less than a week later. As usual, in the end, it was better because my team had more time to prepare. They asked thoughtful questions and focused more closely on process. The time also allowed me to demonstrate that I wasn't leaving because I couldn't wait to get out, but because I listened to my *heart.*

Karyn Pettigrew

SECTION FOUR

Looking at yourself

DO YOU HAVE THE BLAHS?

When we shut down our own vibrancy and spontaneity because we are afraid of being disappointed or embarrassed, or when we follow the status quo because it worked for others, we move away from our true selves and move into a state of "blah." Think about your orientation to life. Do you see it as an exciting journey? Or do you constantly see only the challenges, feeling like you can't succeed unless you work hard and sacrifice, and then, only if you're lucky?

Every time we have a negative experience, we contract, at least for a moment. The detrimental effect comes when we fail to release and expand back to our true form. How do we know when we're contracted? When we begin to shy away from the things we might want to try or look interesting. When we lose our curiosity or sense of adventure. Like anything else, if you stay in one position long enough, you can become stuck there. For instance, every time we try a new sport, interview for a new job, audition for a part in a play, or ask someone out on a date, we are being curious or adventurous. We are taking a risk.

But over time, if we meet with enough negative outcomes, we will want to protect ourselves.

Very often that protection means pulling back our curiosity. The self-talk, the path to mediocrity, goes something like this, *"I don't want to feel that pain again, so I won't even set myself up to possibly feel it. Risks are called risks because they don't carry guarantees. I would be safer if I following a proven path."*

The amazing thing about mediocrity is that it is likely to keep you safer. Following a previously-traveled proven path with

Karyn Pettigrew

success may get you to a fairly mature point in your life. I call it the "good-enough perspective." There's nothing wrong with this perspective as long as it is *truly your perspective*. Problems arise when you have adopted this perspective, but don't really want it, or it's not really yours. When you want something with your heart, but intellectually choose something else, you create a separation between the heart and the mind. You come out of body, mind, spirit alignment. When we exist in that dichotomy for an extended period of time, we begin to experience stress.

Stress occurs when we're pulled away from what we want to do, what we are comfortable with, or what we're willing to do. Our spirits have ways of sending messages about the stress that we're experiencing. I call them our signals. The signals let us know there's something that we need to attend to, that something is out of alignment. Anything that shows up as discontent or discomfort is letting us know we need to take a closer look at what's going on. The effects of stress may manifest in one or more of the following ways:

- Intellectually—Off, or even, poor work performance.
- Physically – A physical ailment or development of an illness.
- Emotionally – Moodiness, a "blah" feeling, or depression.

Stress has many possible triggers. Driving on the expressway may cause me to break out in a cold sweat, but for you, it may be as close to a NASCAR raceway as you're going to get, and you love it. Whatever the trigger, the ability to achieve relief from the stress is universal and can generally be self-managed through choice. If you are experiencing a dramatic change in your ability to manage in your home or work environment, or a change in your normal physical condition, I recommend that you seek professional help.

I QUIT

Choices are not always easy, but we always have more than one, and at least one of them will result in greater personal peace. The choice that will lead us there is the one where

- we have been truthful to ourselves and others;
- we hold the intention to trust ourselves;
- we have been responsible by lovingly acting on our truth.

Are you feeling uncomfortable? Blah? In what area? Intellectual? Physical? Emotional? Spiritual? Are you experiencing stress? Can you identify the cause? What would you prefer to be experiencing? The next section begins to look at these questions. The Aspect Review will look at your intellectual, physical, emotional, and spiritual alignment so that you can map out a plan to get rid of the blahs.

WHAT IS IMPORTANT TO YOU NOW, IN THE PRESENT?

"Presence teaches that what you do today is important because you are trading a day of your life for it."

Dan Millman,
Laws of Spirit[4]

Just what does it mean to "be present"? Why is it better to be present? The present is the only *real time*. We can do nothing about the past except attempt to relive it, and in doing so, reduce the opportunity to address what is in front of us now. The same is true for the future. When we spend time focused on "what ifs" or trying to control every aspect of a future outcome, we are distracted from what is happening now. This does not mean that you shouldn't plan for the future; it simply means not to hold out exclusively for the future. If you are truthful, loving and responsible to yourself right now, you will begin to see the possibilities that exist right now. In addressing what is before you now, you set the direction for the future.

The average American lives to be 76 years old. This sounds like a long time until you realize that somewhere around age 25 we begin to trade off our days. Until that age we tend to live in the present, enjoying life, trying things, being more spontaneous. When we get married, have children, or reach a certain level of responsibility in our jobs it seems a specially coded message unveils itself in our subconscious. The message says, "Get serious now. Be an adult." The word *joy* is extracted from our vocabulary until such time as we have paid the appropriate dues–like at retirement. We become increasingly risk- adverse. It's understandable. We don't want to jeopardize our family, or in some cases, our status or power.

But when we decide to get serious, we tend to lose all creativity and shut ourselves down with all of the reasons why we *cannot* do something instead of looking for a responsible way to make it happen.

This whole inverse relationship of age to fun is a myth! We can still enjoy life and do things that bring us joy as individuals, while co-creating our lives with others. Just as you would extend yourself to be of service to your friends and family, consider extending the same courtesy to yourself. Think about the sense of satisfaction you feel when you know that you have somehow helped someone else. Now project that same energy to yourself. You can live a more joyous, peaceful life, but it starts with knowing what you want *today*. You must know what your truths are—today, not yesterday – or what we think it may be tomorrow. This process will work if you are willing to go in and see what rests in your heart today.

We will start the process by reviewing four aspects that contribute to who you are: intellectual aspect, physical aspect, emotional aspect, and spiritual aspect.

The intellectual aspect is the part of you that relates mostly to your physical functioning throughout the day. It rules the mechanics of your life, the logical, practical aspect. For most people, it can be associated with the work you do.

The physical aspect has two components, the state of your physical body, or health, and the state of your physical environments – your place of work or your home.

The emotional aspect includes the part of you that rules your personal relationships. It is also the part of you that manages your demeanor.

The spiritual aspect is that part of you that is responsible for acknowledging and maintaining a relationship with a higher power beyond ourselves. This is the part that helps to ground you and connect you to humanity.

When these aspects are in balance, you are in alignment and can harness your greatest power.

The next section begins the Alignment Review. It is a tool that you can use to identify and refine what you truly want in each aspect of your life. There will be a guided meditation and reflective questions for you to use. Take your time and be patient with yourself as you delve into aligning with your soul.

ALIGNMENT REVIEW OVERVIEW

Alignment of your four aspects—intellect, body, emotions, and spirit – is the way to get the most out of your life. It results in your greatest power because when you are aligned, you are whole. You are best prepared to address anything that comes your way. Alignment, however, requires a willingness to live in a state of truth, trust, and responsibility for yourself.

Alignment is about bringing ourselves into a natural flow. To be in alignment you must stop fighting yourself; it takes much less energy to flow than to resist. Just think of how hard it is to walk upstream, or against the wind. You must stop resisting the exciting things to which you are drawn and embrace them. Opening to what rests in your heart will reveal your greatest gifts, and sharing those gifts will bring you joy.

The following series of questions looks at the four aspects of you. The questions are designed to help determine what you want today. Your heart, not your mind, should be the source of your responses.

Since, many of us have never really expanded our feelings vocabulary, we tend to overuse the words *nice, okay, fine,* and *good.*

I encourage you to expand the use of your adjectives to include more definitive words. Following is a list to get you started.

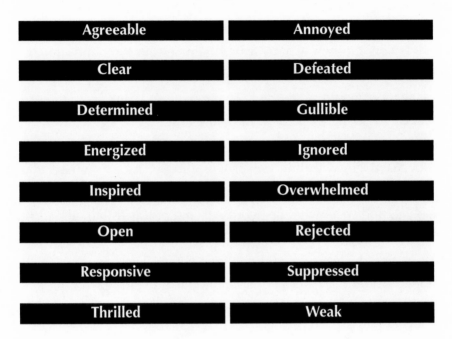

Agreeable	Annoyed
Clear	Defeated
Determined	Gullible
Energized	Ignored
Inspired	Overwhelmed
Open	Rejected
Responsive	Suppressed
Thrilled	Weak

There are three steps to this process, 1) clarify what dreams are right for you; 2) identify the limitations that keep you from accomplishing your dreams; 3) take action to resolve the limitations.

By clarifying what is important to have in your life, you can begin to identify ways to get there. We want to reduce the faceless discomfort and unease that stalks from behind. By shining light on what you want, you can expose the discomfort for what it is, an illusion of weakness.

MEDITATION FOR ALIGNMENT REVIEW

I recommend using the following meditation before you begin the review of each aspect. It will help set the tone and prepare your conscious mind for the work you will be doing. Taping the meditation would be helpful. That way, you won't have to read and try to do the exercise at the same time.

The meditation will only take about five minutes for each aspect. Begin with any aspect you choose. As you answer the questions, it is important that you answer truthfully from a place of feeling, and write what first comes to mind. It is usually the most honest representation of how you feel. I also recommend answering the Aspect questions in a quiet place where you will not be disturbed. Find a comfortable place to sit. Place both feet on the floor. Close your eyes, take three deep breaths, then begin.

Allow yourself to focus on the aspect of your life you are working on. Feel the capacity to see what you truly want and the courage to enact the necessary changes. Trust that you have the ability to make changes in your life that will lead you to greater joy.

Imagine that you are surrounded by white light. You begin to walk forward. In the distance you see a large shape. You feel a pulse. As you move closer you see that it's a door. You realize that the pulse matches your heart beat. You know that this is the doorway to your heart. On the other side lie the answers you seek. When you open the door you will see this aspect of your life as you would like to experience it. Now open the door. Observe everything. Feel how wonderful it is to experience your life as you want it. How do you look? How do you feel? Is anyone here with you? What are they doing? When you feel like you have received all of your message, give thanks and once again, see yourself surrounded by a white, comforting light. When you are ready, open your eyes and write what you experienced. Then answer the questions.

I QUIT

ALIGNMENT REVIEW EXERCISE

Following are the worksheets for the Alignment Review. All of the questions should be answered without censure, even if you feel well-aligned in a particular aspect. You might be surprised at what comes up.

Intellectual Aspect

What is your job? (career, vocation, activities, duties)

A) How do you feel overall about your job? (Refer to the feeling list on page 66)

_____

_____

Is that your *truth*, or does that represent what you *should* say?

_____

_____

B) What would you do, change, or do differently *right now*, if you knew there would be no repercussions and/or no failure?

_____

_____

C) How will those changes expand your life? What actions would you enjoy?

_____

_____

D) State those changes in an affirmative statement of priority. Begin it as, *"It is a priority for me to..."* If you don't have any changes you'd like to make, simply state what it is about the aspect that contributes to your joy.

_____

_____

E) Consider how you can begin to live your priority statement within the context of your current life. What can you do to initiate the change?

_____

_____

I QUIT

Physical Aspect - Personal

How would you describe your personal physical state? (health, level of physical activity, appearance)

A) How do you feel about your physical state? (Refer to the feelings list) _____

_____

Is that your *truth*, or does that represent what you *should* say?

_____

_____

B) What would you do, change, or do differently *right now* if you knew there could be no repercussions and/or no failure?

_____

_____

C) How will those changes expand your life? What actions would you enjoy?

_____

_____

D) State those changes in an affirmative statement of priority. Begin it as, *"It is a priority for me to..."* If there are no changes you'd like to make, simply state what it is about the aspect that contributes to your joy

_____

_____

E) Consider how you can begin to live your priority statement within the context of your current life. What can you do to initiate the change?

_____

_____

Karyn Pettigrew

Physical Aspect – Environment

How would you describe the physical environments in which you spend the most time? (home, work)

A) How do you feel about the physical environment?

_____

_____

Is that your *truth*, or does that represent what you *should* say?

_____

_____

B) What would you do, change, or do differently *right now* if you knew there could be no repercussions and/or no failure?

_____

_____

C) How will those changes expand your life? What actions would you enjoy?

_____

_____

D) State those changes in an affirmative statement of priority. Begin it as, *"It is a priority for me to...."* If there are no changes you'd like to make, simply state what it is about the aspect that contributes to your joy.

_____

_____

E) Consider how you can begin to live your priority statement within the context of your current life. What can you do to initiate the change?

_____

_____

I QUIT

Emotional Aspect

Select a relationship to begin with.

A) How do you feel about the relationship? (relationship, commitments)

_____

_____

Is that your *truth*, or does that represent what you *should* say?

_____

_____

B) What would you do, change, or do differently *right now* if there could be no repercussions and/or no failure?

_____

_____

C) How will those changes expand your life? What actions would you enjoy?

_____

_____

D) State those changes in an affirmative statement of priority. Begin it as, *"It is a priority for me to..."* If there are no changes you'd like to make, simply state what it is about the aspect that contributes to your joy.

_____

_____

E) Consider how you can begin to live your priority statement within the context of your current life. What can you do to initiate the change?

_____

_____

Karyn Pettigrew

Spiritual Aspect

How do you connect to a sense of the greater-beyond-you? (rejuvenating aspects, purpose, inspiration, service)

A) How do you feel about the connection?

_____

_____

Is that your *truth*, or does that represent what you *should* say?

_____

_____

B) What would you, do, change, or do differently *right now*, if you knew there could be no repercussions and/or no failure?

_____

_____

C) How will those changes expand your life? What actions would you enjoy?

_____

_____

D) State those changes in an affirmative statement of priority. Begin it as, *"It is a priority for me to..."* If there are no changes you'd like to make, simply state what it is about the aspect that contributes to your joy.

_____

_____

E) Consider how you can begin to live your priority statement within the context of your current life. What can you do to initiate the change?

_____

_____

REVIEW OF YOUR ANSWERS TO
THE ALIGNMENT EXERCISE

Notice how you feel about each aspect. Any negative feelings indicate a place for realignment or change. One of the first steps in moving toward full alignment is for you to simply understand the source of your discomfort.

Question A.

How do you feel? What do you honestly believe? Is that your truth?

Your feelings are the indicators of your alignment with your beliefs. For instance, you feel angry or frustrated because you stay late at work each night. Your belief is that you should stay. Your feelings of anger or frustration are a signal that you are not in agreement with this belief.

You filter every thought through your beliefs before you *do* anything, so that ultimately, your feelings, not your thoughts, direct you toward your truth. Knowing what you feel, and then accepting those feelings, is not a practice we have generally been encouraged to pursue, especially when what you feel is counter to conventional wisdom. Please note that accepting a feeling is not equivalent to living it, especially negative feelings. Accepting is simply an acknowledgement of the feeling. Once acknowledged you want to move on and stay in the flow.

Let's say you were involved in a three-car collision. No one was hurt, but all three cars were badly damaged. You may feel in shock, angry, disappointed, and blaming. These feelings are an experience of the moment, not a state of being. Acknowledgement of the feelings gives you a place from which to move. Using this example, you may have been in shock, but once you know everyone is okay, you can move on. You felt anger and blame because one of the other cars ran a red light. You can redirect that energy right into the police and insurance reports. You might have felt disappointed because the trunk of your car was smashed, but you can release that, too, because the reports have been filed, and you can't do anything until the body shop gets back to you. In the end, the event is over, there is no "re-do." It's energetically more beneficial to stay in the forward flow of "doing the next thing," or "the next steps" than to resist by stewing in negativity. Continuing to spend your energy on those emotions is draining and unconstructive.

The fuel for movement toward alignment is our feelings. Anything you noted about how you *should* feel deserves reflection and comparison to how you *do* feel. *Should-feels* are rarely sourced by our own desires. Carrying out *should do's* often set us up for stress – doing something uncomfortable. Some stress is good; it can lead us to personal growth like when trying something for the first time. Prolonged stress is unhealthy and distracts from our personal center. Try to separate your own feelings from others for each aspect of your life.

Question B.
What would you change if you could not fail?

Exploration of this question will bring you to your truth. At this point, it is what you would prefer to be experiencing. Try not to limit your exploration of this question. Really give yourself permission to feel deeply about what you want. How far do you dare to go? Only you set your limits, but remember that this is about you. It is not about imposing your will on another. Although all processes are co-creative, if your dream involves another, they must meet you there. You create imbalance when you attempt to manipulate someone into your vision of your life. Rarely will it come out the way you plan.

Question C.
How will the changes expand your life? What actions would you enjoy?

When you identify how the changes expand your life, you begin to lay out and envision a more balanced, harmonious state. You begin to create blueprints. You move your energy forward.

Your imagination is the starting point for creating the life you envision. It's the source of your power. You must imagine before you can achieve. See it first and then add layers to your vision. How do these changes allow you to operate through your day? How do you feel with the changes in place? Go deeply into the possibilities. It is from this place that you will identify your actions.

Action D.
State the changes in an affirmative statement of priority.

By stating the changes you identified in an affirmative statement of priority, you consciously and sub-consciously establish a goal. "It is now a priority for me to..."

You are making a commitment to yourself, one that physically puts what you *will* out into the world. You are committing energetic resources to making the changes happen.

Question E.

What can you do to initiate change?

Think about how you could initiate the changes. You don't have to make grand, sweeping changes in the beginning. In fact, I would recommend doing just the opposite. Take the first, easy step and progress toward larger, more difficult changes. Working this way accomplishes two things. First, it is less stressful and may be less traumatic for you. Second, it will build your confidence as you experience initial successes. Each success makes it easier to move on to larger changes.

By reviewing the answers to your Alignment Review, you will see your truth. This is who you are. Can you find it in the work you do? You must be able to find these truths and these enabling features in the way you spend your time daily. Otherwise, you will eventually find that your lifestyle does not support you.

Experiencing balance in our lives should not be seen as a luxury. It is an entitlement. The challenge to achieving it rests with us. On the next page is your alignment wheel. Fill it in with your responses to questions B, D and E for each aspect. This forms the basis for the things you want fully present in your life.

Your life is dynamic; what you want, need, and desire will change over time. You can use this exercise any time you feel blocked or want clarity.

ALIGNMENT WHEEL

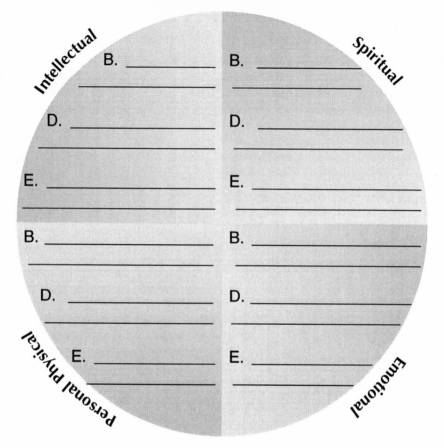

Environmental Physical

B. _____

D. _____

E. _____

Karyn Pettigrew

SECTION FIVE

Making it happen

EXPAND YOUR BOUNDARIES

Do you know what the sky looked like this morning? Can you remember? You may not care. It's not critical information, but it's interesting. Have you eaten a meal with someone you love recently, not in front of the TV, and not *on the fly*? In the past two days? In the past week? Two weeks? Have you told someone this week that you love them? How recently have you have been told that you are loved?

I make this point not to judge, criticize, or reprimand. I make the point to illustrate that we must choose to align our lives. We must put back what is important. No one is going to magically clear the way for us. There is much that competes for our time and attention. What to do? How can you live differently? Of course you must work to support yourself and your family. It's the responsible thing to do. But I propose that you can do your work more joyously with a shift in perspective and a redefinition of boundaries. Instead of seeing boundaries as a place to set limits, consider them as points on the horizon. How far can you expand?

When I think of the perspective many of us take of our work, it seems we feel not so much *in-service* as *enslaved*. We have enslaved ourselves by failing to recognize our free will and power to choose. We have reduced our value to an index of the work we do and how hard we work at it. There is nothing wrong with hard work or even losing yourself in it periodically, so long as it's fortifying you. However, when it is not what you want, there is grumbling and complaining; we become victims, martyrs, or rescuers. We forget about our power to choose. The truth is that we have choice opportunities at every turn. There are limitless opportunities to change direction. We have no boundaries to our potential.

Amelia felt miserable. Everything was a struggle and way out of hand. She was taking medication every day. Despite holding a top position with a national organization, she was constantly required to prove herself with little support from her peers or management. She found herself multi-tasking constantly. She was on call 24 hours a day and traveled every week. As a result, she completely lost control over her personal time.

About a year into the position, Amelia began looking for an executive coach to help her negotiate the corporate waters and provide insight on regaining balance in her life. Once, during a conversation with a coach, she was riding an exercise bike while working on a hand-held computer. It was too much. She strongly felt the need to change. Amelia recognized that she went to the coach suspecting she would quit her job. In fact, she did. The process of resigning generated anger among the group that had come to rely on her ability to, "get the job done, in a hurry." Despite this, Amelia experienced great relief. She felt energized after being separated from her sense of personal power for so long. She had regained her power to choose.

Amelia considers one of her greatest lessons from this experience is *reclaiming the power* that comes with knowing who she is, loving who she is, and honoring her ability to choose. She is no longer a victim.

Today, Amelia works as a personal coach and business consultant. Her own coaching experience as a client helped her realize that she wanted to help others regain their personal power in professional settings. Coaching allows Amelia to do what she

I QUIT

had been doing all along, creating business solutions, but this time through the empowerment of others.

"Managing your Boundaries," is a practice that has been pointed to as a way to preserve our health and save our lives. *Webster's New World Dictionary and Thesaurus* defines a boundary as, *"anything marking a limit, bound."* The thesaurus lists other nouns such as: outline, beginning, end, confines, limits, and horizon. This is interesting because most of today's discussions about personal boundaries focus on establishing them to prevent encroachment, to keep out. Instead, I propose that we need to manage our *commitments* and expand our *boundaries*. See the possibilities while remembering that more does not always mean better.

The law of diminishing returns supports this idea, and it carries as much force in our lives as it does in economic theory. It states:

"If one factor of production is increased while others remain constant, the overall returns will relatively decrease after a certain point[5]."

This law was originally conceived to address agricultural scenarios; it was later accepted as an economic law applicable to all production ventures. When translated to the language of this book, the law of diminishing return reads something like this:

"If we increase the amount of time and effort that we dedicate to the work we do, while our day remains fixed at a 24-hour maximum, the overall quality and quantity of our work will eventually decrease after a certain point."

We could give more and more of our day over to our work, but at some point the work will suffer, and ultimately the reasons that you put in so much time (money, status, power) will be jeopardized as well. If you have ever "pulled an all-nighter," you know what I'm referring to–exhaustion. Exhaustion comes in several flavors, not just physical, but mental, emotional, and spiritual as well. We need to re-energize with food, rest, and, yes, fun.

No one can encroach upon our boundaries unless we allow it. Setting boundaries for ourselves is really like setting limits to our potential. Instead, consider expanding your boundaries, extending your experiences, and therefore, the definition of You. No matter who you think you are, you are so much more.

Simultaneously, limit your commitments. Pull back from the things that result in negative emotions. Push out toward those activities or experiences that enrich, nurture and energize you – the places you thought you would never go.

MANAGE YOUR COMMITMENTS

Many people give more than 50 percent of their day to the work they do. To align fully, you must examine what you get out of a commitment that requires so much from you. Do you know why you're signed up for all the committees, organizations, and teams? What kinds of returns are you looking for? What do you expect? I encourage you to think beyond monetary rewards. What does satisfaction mean for you?

Every time you do something that someone else feels you "should" do, you trade away your vitality. I am *not* saying never do things that others recommend or think we should do. We often get helpful suggestions from others. I am asking you to be aware that when you do something solely at someone else's direction, it doesn't serve you. Realize you have choices. I call it the Stop, Drop, or Roll menu. For everything that you have committed yourself to, consider the following options:

1) Stop – doing it yourself and gracefully decline further participation.
2) Drop – it into the capable hands of a surrogate.
3) Roll with it – do it anyway,

Richard was extremely over-committed. His willingness to help others and his committed follow-through often resulted in many requests for assistance. As a public defender he worked long hours. He was on three not-for-profit boards and was the primary caregiver of an ailing aunt. Besides these regular commitments, his friends and family often called on him for help. Richard was exhausted. Although he wanted to help, he never had time to regenerate. He eventually saw that his commitments had become

Karyn Pettigrew

burdensome. He began to lose sight of himself; so he knew he had to review each of his commitments. He began with the not-for-profits. While he respected them all, he realized that none was getting his best efforts. He resigned from all but one. He also took a look at and deepened his willingness to say no. As friends and family asked him to help, he was truthful about his ability to do so, and would often suggest another person or ways they could complete the task by themselves. He was particularly watchful of requests that would put something of importance to him on hold.

Take an inventory of your commitments. Notice those activities that bring you joy and those you consider a hassle. Do this for all the ways you give of yourself at work or at home.

Spend some time and write out for each day of the week all of the ways that you've committed yourself–intellectually, physically, emotionally and spiritually. Next to each item write either an "M" for My choices or an "S" for Someone else's. Refer to your Alignment Wheel to see if the items you've marked "M" support how you would like to be living your life. The ones that do not support your vision need to be postponed or released. The items marked "S" must be carefully considered. Why have you committed yourself to someone else's vision? Do you want to be part of it? If so, how does participating support your vision?

Using the charts on the following pages, make a list of your time commitments for each day of the week. Then in the third column indicate why you do it. Be honest – this is your life. Try to determine if the hassle outweighs the joy. If the activity is too much of a hassle consider the stop, drop or roll menu.

I QUIT

COMMITMENT EXERCISE SHEET

Day _____

Time	What You Do	Why You Do It	Hassle or Joy	Stop	Drop	Roll

COMMITMENT EXERCISE SHEET

Day _____

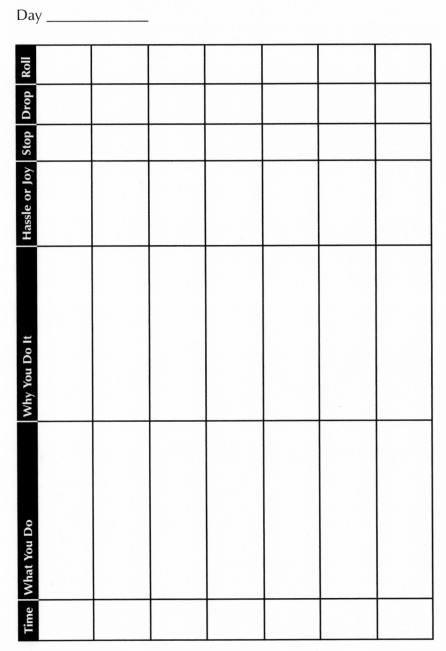

Time	What You Do	Why You Do It	Hassle or Joy	Stop	Drop	Roll

I QUIT

COMMITMENT EXERCISE SHEET

Day _____

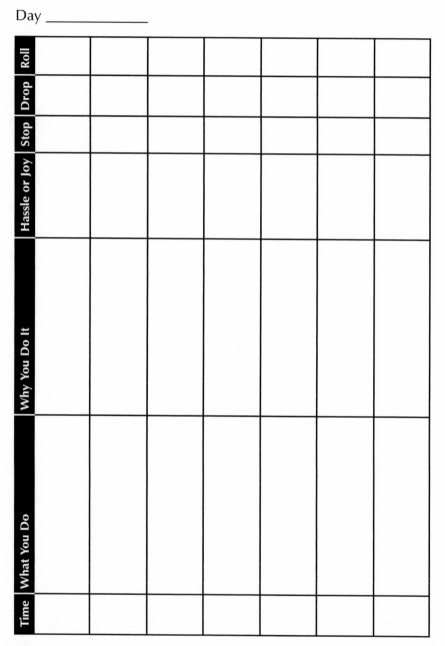

Time	What You Do	Why You Do It	Hassle or Joy	Stop	Drop	Roll

Karyn Pettigrew

COMMITMENT EXERCISE SHEET

Day _____

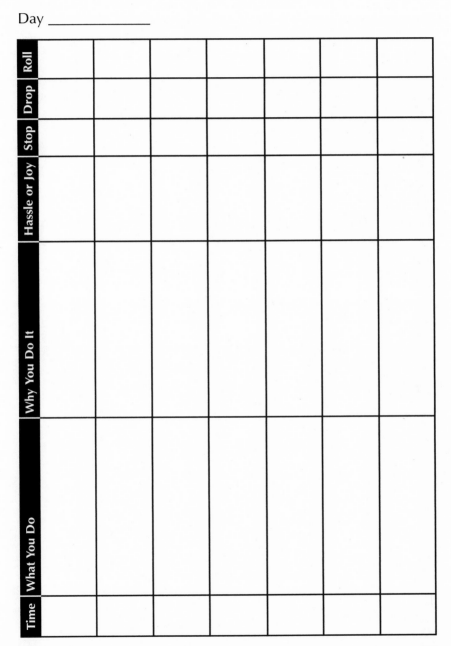

Time	What You Do	Why You Do It	Hassle or Joy	Stop	Drop	Roll

Karyn Pettigrew

I QUIT

COMMITMENT EXERCISE SHEET

Day _____

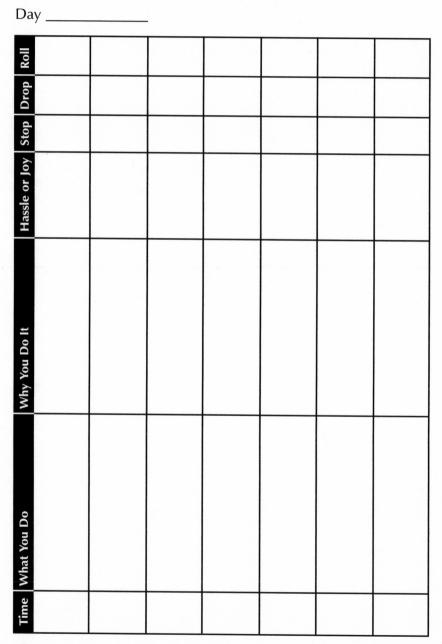

Roll						
Drop						
Stop						
Hassle or Joy						
Why You Do It						
What You Do						
Time						

Karyn Pettigrew

COMMITMENT EXERCISE SHEET

Day _____

Time	What You Do	Why You Do It	Hassle or Joy	Stop	Drop	Roll

Karyn Pettigrew

I QUIT

COMMITMENT EXERCISE SHEET

Day _____

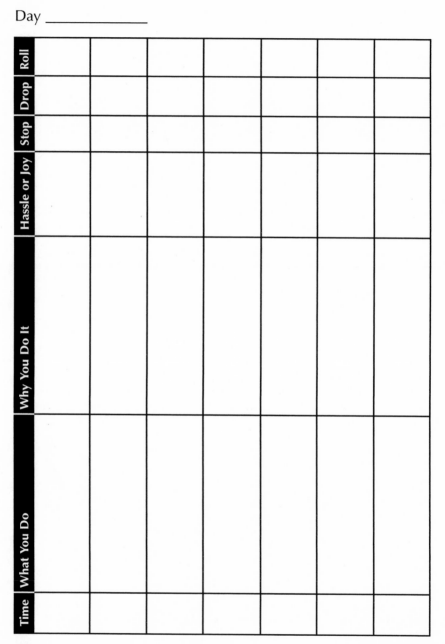

Time	What You Do	Why You Do It	Hassle or Joy	Stop	Drop	Roll

Karyn Pettigrew

STOP COMPLAINING

We've all been wounded; it's inevitable. From the first time we're told no, we learn about restrictions and we begin to know what it's like to have our choices made by someone else. Now, this is not to say that we should be allowed to do anything we want, whenever we want, especially children, but it is to say that we have been learning about limitations and the experience of lack for a long time. For most people, the apparent inevitability of lack becomes a veiled belief, one that we don't even notice is there. We live with it each day, filtering our perceptions and experiences.

One of the most effective ways to positively affect your life is to stop complaining. When you stop complaining you stop wasting good energy on negative thoughts. It's like putting a clean-air filter on your psyche. When you stop complaining you automatically begin to *clean your house*. You've heard the phrase, "you are what you eat," well, you are also what you think and how you behave.

One of the most self-sabotaging things you can do is to commit time and energy to complaining. If you complain to yourself and to others, you are perpetuating negative thoughts and behavior. You devote more energy to negative action than progressive, expansive action. You also give your power away. When you complain you take on the role of victim and surrender your power to someone else.

If you complain a lot about one thing, or if you complain a little about a lot of things, others will feel its okay to come to you and join your chorus of complaints.

Karyn Pettigrew   95

I QUIT

A complaint, like pain is usually a signal that something is out of alignment. As with pain, we can just treat the symptom or address the cause. Treating the symptom rarely results in long-term improvement. To address the cause, we must first learn to identify our complaints for the warning signals that they are. A complaint can be productive if it acts as a stimulus for constructive change. Keywords that signal when you're in the midst of a complaint are *never, always, only*. By themselves, these are not bad words, but when used in the context of a complaint, they create energetic poison. The following chart outlines some examples:

Phrase	Lack	Alternative Perspective
I'll never get a chance...	Lack of opportunity	What can I do to create an opportunity?
He always rejects my proposals...	Lack of acceptance	I should ask him what he is looking for in a proposal.
They'll never agree with this idea...	Lack of agreement	First, I should confirm that they agree that we have an issue.
My mother only listens to my brother's suggestions	Lack of credibility	Perhaps my brother and I should present the idea.

All perceptions of lack ultimately point to a perspective of our inability to create what we want or need. The perceptions usually reflect what we feel we do not have. If we do not attempt to take action to change it, we end up in a perceived victim mode. All of the Alternative Perspective suggestions listed above require responsible action. Use the following exercise to list your complaints and determine what you can do to start and maintain forward momentum.

COMPLAINING EXERCISE

You can begin by listing five things that you complain about. Good examples include the use of *always, never or only.* Consider the things that bug you. Try to identify the "indication of lack" that each complaint addresses and then consider an alternative perspective (action) you can take.

EXAMPLE: <u>My spouse never helps with the housework.</u>
Indication of lack (what I don't have/what I want): <u>Time for myself.</u>
Alternative perspective I can take: <u>a) talk to my spouse about helping, b) hire someone to help.</u>

1) _____
Indication of lack: _____
Alternative perspective I can take:_____

2) _____
Indication of lack _____
Alternative perspective I can take:_____

3) _____
Indication of lack _____
Alternative perspective I can take:_____

4) _____
Indication of lack _____
Alternative perspective I can take:_____

5) _____
Indication of lack _____
Alternative perspective I can take:_____

I QUIT

BLAMING AND COMPLAINING – CONJOINED TWINS

Like complaining, blaming sends your energy to a dead end. It's the same as using faulty material when building a house. It weakens the project. Blaming moves beyond the simple cause and effect, to an experience of lack. It acts as a negative energy boomerang. I blame you, but the discomfort swings back to me.

The boomerang effect can be avoided if we focus on moving forward and doing the next thing to remedy the negative experience. Blame, lagging behind looking for fault, resists the flow. Let's go back to the three-car accident example. The simple cause and effect is that a car ran a red light which led to the pile-up. There are myriad actions that can be taken from this point to move forward: call the police; call the insurance company; call the spouse for a ride home; etc.

When we blame, we stay focused on the person or event that caused us to feel shocked, angry, and disappointed. As awful as the scenario was, it's over. Can you see how spending time recycling the information gets you nowhere? Going round and round about how stupid the driver's actions were gets you nowhere. There's no forward flow.

Blaming is a lack of responsibility for the self – the responsibility to move forward in every situation. Take a few moments to list some of the people or situations where you place blame. Then try to identify the action you can take to move forward out of the stalemate of blame.

I BLAME _____

FOR CAUSING_____

_____

WHAT I WANT (desired result) _____

_____

I CAN MOVE FORWARD BY _____

_____

I BLAME _____

FOR CAUSING_____

_____

WHAT I WANT (desired result) _____

_____

I CAN MOVE FORWARD BY _____

_____

I BLAME _____

FOR CAUSING_____

_____

WHAT I WANT (desired result) _____

_____

I CAN MOVE FORWARD BY _____

_____

I BLAME _____

FOR CAUSING_____

_____

WHAT I WANT (desired result) _____

_____

I CAN MOVE FORWARD BY _____

_____

ASK FOR WHAT YOU WANT

The natural corollary to the cessation of complaining and blaming is to ask for what you want. I have already said that to manifest positive things in your life you must change your perspective. When you want to complain or blame, stop yourself, turn it around, and *ask for what you want*. This works well with other people, too. When they come to you to complain – stop them and ask what they would like instead. The effect is amazing.

Again, a complaint is a signal from our internal sensors that we are experiencing discomfort or discontent. By stopping to identify it, we are giving ourselves an opportunity to redirect the energy in a more positive way. It works across the spectrum of situations; it even works with children.

My 6-year-old daughter would often start her complaint with, "Mom, you never let me have my friends over." Having friends over is a constant request. However, she was not feeling any control over her play dates. She wasn't playing with her friends as much as she'd like. Regardless of whether the complaint was based on factual information, she felt powerless. Her accusation automatically put me on the opposing side. One of my teachers, Sonia Choquette often reminds me to ignore our differences and see how we are alike and to look for the opportunity to create together.

The solution is to operate from a perspective of possibilities. To see the "what if?" in every situation. A complaint has too much potential for dead-ending, while asking for what you want is filled with possibility.

I responded to my daughter by telling her to ask for what she wanted instead of complaining about what she didn't have. Instantly, her facial expression changed. She brightened up and asked if we could set up more play dates to which I agreed. Two things are important about this exchange. First, by asking for what she wanted she was in the perspective of possibility. Operating from possibility is infinitely more fun and a better tool for relationships. By taking the perspective of possibility, we become co-creators. I was more willing to respond as a partner in making play dates happen for her as opposed to a taking a defensive posture when I've been accused of "never allowing her to have friends over."

The same exchange is true for any scenario involving co-workers or personal relationships. Complaining is a demonstration of fear–the lack of control over ourselves. Sometimes we try to protect ourselves from that fear by predicting a negative outcome. We protect ourselves from being let down. If the negative prediction comes true, we may feel justified in our complaint, but we have gained no additional control. Fear of being without is like having molten lead poured in your legs. It is heavy and dense and when it cools is no longer malleable. By operating from a place of possibilities, you keep the outcome flowing, even if the first answer is not exactly what you wanted. Consider this example.

Amanda was the project manager assigned to coordinate the launch of a corporate Web site at a large company. At the time, Amanda was responsible for several big projects. Over time, she discovered that maintaining and updating the site required as much as 10-20 hours of her time each week. She complained about the staff writers who never seemed to prioritize the Web articles. She had complaints about upper management not prioritizing the Web projects. She was also concerned about the complexity of the work increasing as the site became more and more interactive. I asked Amanda if she had asked for what she wanted. She hadn't. Finally, instead of sitting with the complaints, she wrote up what she needed.

Amanda suggested that the department hire a content manager who could be the point person for information coming from the various departments, while also working with IT on maintaining the site. The content manager could even write articles for the site when necessary. Her boss presented the write-up to the vice-president, who after some consideration, said no to the new hire, but supported better utilization of the staff that was available.

Perhaps some would see this as a failure since Amanda didn't get exactly what she wanted. But by asking for what she wanted, instead of complaining about what she didn't have, Amanda received forward motion. By voicing her needs, Amanda co-created a revised process that better utilized the writers and assigned the daily maintenance to another person. All of this reduced the hours required of her on this project, which was her goal. By voicing what she wanted Amanda also heightened the sensitivity of all parties involved to be on the lookout for the time when a full-time person would be appropriate.

RIDDING YOURSELF OF FEARS

If you are experiencing fear around asking for what you want, or if you are considering taking action that causes you fear, try the following exercise to help you take your power back from your fears. Fear is nothing but the feeling that you are incapable of handling something. Think about it.

Facing the fear - Exercise

Write down three things that you are afraid might happen if you take action toward your joy.

THREE THINGS THAT I AM AFRAID MIGHT HAPPEN IF I TAKE ACTION TOWARD MY JOY:

1) _____

2) _____

3) _____

I QUIT

I recommend taping the following meditation. Add soothing instrumental music in the background if you'd like. Find a comfortable place to sit where you will not be disturbed and begin.

MEDITATION FOR FACING THE FEAR

As you close your eyes, take three deep breaths. As you exhale the last deep breath, imagine that a gold ball of light descends from the sky and surrounds you. You realize that you are now inside the gold ball. The walls are a transparent swirl of iridescent gold, pink, and white. This ball will serve as a safe harbor while you consider the source of your fears. In this safe, nurturing place consider your first fear. Place the energy of that fear in a beautiful sack. Close it and push the sack through the iridescent wall. Let the sack go. It is now released. The negative energy will be recycled to positive energy. Now consider what you would like to experience instead of the fear. Hold that positive vision of what you want in your mind and in your heart. Now ask, through your connection to God, your higher self, or whatever greater source you consider, for directions on how to make your vision happen. You may see a picture, hear or see words, but be quiet and patient and a response will come.

Do this again for each of your fears. When you have asked about all three fears, give thanks for your connection and slowly open your eyes.

Immediately write down the direction that you were given. Try not to censor or judge the response you get. Spirit is subtle. It may not be a complete solution, but you should get some insight to help move you forward.

RECORD THE DIRECTION YOU WERE GIVEN IN THE MEDITATION

Fear 1 direction: _____

_____

Fear 2 direction: _____

_____

Fear 3 direction: _____

_____

FIND YOUR INSPIRATION – WHY YOU DO IT

Once you have prioritized your commitments, eliminated complaining, and begun to ask for what you really want, you can better evaluate your work for how well it supports you. The support comes in the form of inspiration. Whether it's for your work life or your home life, you need to feel inspired. We all need a unifying element, a bigger picture, to truly find meaning and satisfaction.

In October, 2000, the Work in America Institute (WAI) released a study funded by The Ford Foundation and 15 major corporations and unions centered on strategies companies could use to create better work/life balance and business. The WAI found that:

1) employee involvement (also known as commitment, inspiration) drives innovation and team creativity.

2) companies that take a dual work/life agenda approach achieve significant business results.

3) work/life solutions address many aspects such as reduced work loads, overtime, and stress levels, as well as increased flexibility and time for family and leisure.[6]

Generally, we feel best when we know that we have helped or been of service to someone. When we do things that have no meaning for us, we eventually lose interest and find ourselves just going through the motions. Sometimes we will use our will power to just get us up and through each day, often forcing the smile and just getting the job done. This is terribly draining of energy. It takes much more energy to get us through something that we have little or no desire to do. At the end of the day we are exhausted and lose interest in doing even those few things that bring us joy, further contributing to the negative energy spiral. We can't get to the exercise class, or we don't feel like joining friends for a night out. Playing with the kids seems like hard work.

Make what you do connect with *what lights you up*. Go back to your aspect review. Look for yourself in the work you do. Ask yourself what is my commitment to what I'm doing? How does this make me feel good? How does this satisfy my personal core values?

Ah, core values? If you're in the corporate world, more than likely you've been e-mailed, inner-office mailed, or if you're lucky, attended a live presentation on corporate core values. Those are the attributes that capture a company's character. They include such watchwords as collaborative, innovative, inclusive, honest, accountable, respectful, and adaptable.

The same qualities are relevant for you as a person. What are your core values? Do you know what you believe in? Stand for? If you had a personal crest, what would be on it? Confident? Loving? Kind? Honest? Trustworthy? Whatever they are, they must be with you constantly, in your environment, and in your character, for you to be truly satisfied.

STOP TRYING

" Try not. Do or do not. There is no try."
– Yoda—from Star Wars-The Empire Strikes Back

Stop using the word try, especially in the context of manifestation. To "try to" do something is the same as preparing to do something versus being in the act of doing it. So, if you desire to write a book, never say that you're "trying to write a book." Think, speak, and act like a writer who "is writing a book." Assume the position!

Trying at something allows us to avoid full commitment. We give ourselves room not to complete the action. At this point in the book, you should be clear on the roles and power of focus, intention, and commitment. Be clear on where you put your energy and your commitments. Focus only on those things that serve to enhance and bring to life the vision you hold for yourself. You cannot try at your life. You cannot prepare for it. You are *in* it. You *live it,* actively, every day. Even if it is not yet exactly what you want.

CO-CREATING WITH OTHERS –
KNOW WHY THEY DO IT

If you are working on a specific project or task with others – co-workers, spouse, partner – ask them the same questions: What are they looking for personally? If they were to fast-forward to the end of the project, how would they measure success? How do they want to feel? Be diligent in getting answers; stay away from vague responses. Identifying the actions that bring satisfaction to you and your team members will broaden your awareness for potential opportunities. Those opportunities may lead to a more harmonious outcome.

You can go through the same exercises for a joint project. Use the intellectual aspect template. Compare responses of the participants. Look for places of convergence. What are your teammates looking for? What do they want? Everyone's inspiration statements will form the group's commitment. Understand what people are willing to bring to the proverbial table. If someone cannot find a reason or inspiration, their participation should be reconsidered. It takes passion, commitment, focus, and action to get anything done well. The most successful activities have those ingredients aplenty.

The reason given by each team member for participating is likely to be different. That's okay. No one will feel exactly the same way you do. The art of sucess is in building an inclusive agreement about where the team is going and what each member is willing to contribute. Knowing the various reasons or inspirations for participating will help align people with appropriate roles, prevent misunderstandings, and reduce

I QUIT

potential frustration. Use the commitment lists to be sure the participants are not over-committed, and therefore unable to focus on the project.

MANIFEST WHAT YOU WANT

Once you have agreement and alignment regarding your priorities and desired outcome, it's time to manifest (act on) what you want. To manifest successfully requires several key actions:

Focus: To focus is to bring your full attention to the desired objective of the project. What we spend time thinking about is where our creative energies flow. So, if you spend time focused on how bad something is, you'll create a bad situation because it's what you're expecting.

Commitment (prioritize): When you have cleaned house and made your dream or project a priority, you have cleared away those activities that are more hassle than joy. You have devoted your energy to the perspective of possibilities rather than to unconstructive complaints. It is now that you are demonstrating your commitment to the outcome you seek.

Support: Only include people in your project who are supportive of you. Be wary of support outside of yourself. If you're unavoidably on a project with someone who drains you energetically, look for ways this person can help the group and limit your interaction to only what's necessary. Remember, no one creates alone. It's a virtual impossibility. Let's say you decide to build a special widget in your garage all by yourself. Well, you can't. It's impossible. Someone taught you the necessary steps to build the widget – either a teacher, or an author, or a co-worker. Someone will manufacture the parts you need. Someone built the garage you use as your lab. Farmers and other food manufacturers produce the food you buy at the store to eat and give yourself the energy to work on the widget each day. The chain of co-creation goes on and on. You are never alone, and you never create alone.

Faith: This is the most important of all the steps to manifesting. It feels intangible until you've experienced enough instances of positive manifestations so that you know it works. Whether you believe in support from a higher source, manifesting requires faith in yourself and your powers of creation to keep moving toward your goal each day. Faith is the belief that the solution will come. It is trusting, and then knowing. The key is to remain open to how the solution might look when it arrives, or who the messenger might be. It might not be what you expect. Faith asks you to be at peace with your decision even if you never get external validation that it was the right thing to do. Faith asks you to trust yourself enough to know what you need, and go on in the face of potential rejection because your heart has told you it is right for you.

Faith in yourself will bring you joy and lead a more fulfilling life. You will shift from a "leap of faith" to a "confidence of conscience" as your experiences begin to validate this process.

One of the best books I know for laying out the principles for manifesting in your life is *Your Heart's Desire* by Sonia Choquette. The nine principles Choquette sets forth for attaining your heart's desire are easy to understand, and the exercises and examples are very helpful in reinforcing the concepts. Her work has helped thousands around the world, me included.

ARE YOU STILL FEELING DISCOMFORT?

If you are still experiencing discomfort after you've reviewed your commitment, perspective, and inspiration, reconsider what you want and what other steps might be necessary to take. You may have to change areas of the company, or even change companies. The point is to know who you are by knowing what brings you joy, what inspires you, and what brings you pain. When you know these things you can make decisions that move you toward a continued balance and peace.

If you can't seem to get a handle on it, please seek professional help. There are many professional therapists, counselors, and doctors who can help you sort through persistent blocks.

In our hearts lies a magnificent treasure of dreams, desire, and service. We all ultimately wish to serve the good of others, but often lack the courage to pursue it. I am asking you to be courageous and self-loving as you discover your heart's truth. Feel yourself in your vision. Talk as if it's already done. There is great power in our thoughts and words. Be conscious of it.

EPILOGUE

My personal journey

I QUIT

MY STORY THROUGH THE LAST DAY AT WORK

Following are excerpts from my journal from the time I decided to leave my corporate job to my last day. I have included the journal because I feel it's the most honest illustration of how the process unfolded for me. I mention a few people by name, of course. I know whom I'm referring to, but for your clarification: Carl is my husband; Paul is an evolutionary astrologist; Sonia is one of my teachers.

1/5/02

Yesterday I quit my job. Well, actually I gave notice that I would be leaving in March. It was a much anticipated and agonizing decision. The conversation was great, but the process has been painful over the past few months. I do believe that I needed to be that uncomfortable in order to make the decision that I finally made. There were times before I announced when I felt like, "hum, it's not so bad. I could do this a while longer," and then I'd get a flair up and "remember" how stressful my job could be. Then again, I know (intellectually) that no one can make me feel anything. I have to allow it. I wonder if I quit because I was afraid of failing in a new position. But I'd only fail because it wasn't the right place for me. So, no, all of my cues signal my next act. I feel workshops, presentations, motivational speaking. I want to re-light the fire in people's hearts. Right now, I feel a little relieved, not anxious or afraid. I am trusting, really trusting my heart that this is right. I expect there to be further clarity regarding my "next step." I expect to be guided to the next step. I have surrendered and I am open. I feel like I just need to "be," and to be aware.

1/16/02

I met with Sonia today and she explained that I need to write this experience to understand what I am feeling compelled to do-about being a messenger, telling a story. My meeting with her was insightful and felt in many ways like validation. I had thought about writing a book. I thought that it might be instructional, about living your truth, or finding the passion in your life; finding the everyday person that lives an extraordinary experience through their hearts; taking the limits off and seeing what amazing stories can be told.

Just the other day I saw a PBS special about the man who found the Titanic and his subsequent search of the Black Sea for the perfect shipwreck. He was drawn there by the writings of two other scientists regarding Noah's Ark and the possibility of the remains still being viable in the anoxic layer of the sea. How do people get to the point that they do such amazing things?

The reaction of my peers and co-workers has been bittersweet. Everyone has commented on the loss to the organization–many have commented about my work ethic, my contribution, and how they enjoyed working with me. I wasn't expecting that. I expected them to be nice, curious, to wish me well, but their sincerity has taken me by surprise. The hole that people say they expect to experience after I leave surprises me. I had a conversation with one of the assistants in my area for 25 minutes. She said that how I feel about others finding peace, came through in my attitude. She commented on how many people had nothing but great things to say. (The world is starved for balance)

I know how right this is. She asked for a business card, but I'm not ready to hand out my cards. It doesn't feel quite right yet,

I QUIT

although several people have asked when the doors will open to my Wellness Center.

1/17/02

    I find myself almost compelled to "hold space" for myself and others. I've used that language to help others find a way to live more joyously. All of my experiences are about my "tool kit." Authentically, I can say that "I did it, try it." I've worked up a model and want nothing more than to work with people to identify the blocks and help direct them to their "guides." I want to strengthen my spiritual practice, to tune in and know my inner voice more clearly. I find that each day as people catch me to talk about my leaving, I am more comfortable explaining what I plan to do. I still start with the "brick and mortar" healing center, when I know initially it will be just me.

    Although there are times when I am not sure that I fully believe that I can do it—counsel others and be paid for it. I am a bit reluctant to assume the mastership role for this when the financial piece is attached. So I've stuck to the management aspect in my explanation to people of what I'll be doing. It's been interesting how many people are engaged when I explain. They say things like, "oh, help me" or "I'll come down." I find myself trying to bridge this more logically for people. Again, that's my need to be validated, legitimate to others.

    I show more of myself each day. I now admit to facilitating classes and coaching one-on-one. I think about how surprised people are by how real and in-depth this is for me when I was so clearly occupied in my job. Where did I get the time? How focused on this, yet accomplished at work. I truly appreciate the well-wishes, but I must admit that I have pangs of guilt about

Karyn Pettigrew

leaving. I know how much there is to do in my department.

Last night I left 30 minutes later than I planned because I was talking with a guy in my group about what I planned to do. It just flowed. He had a few questions, then listened as I explained. He commented that he wanted to know more. We are starved to live our truths – authentically.

1/18/02

I had an interesting conversation with my company's leadership consultant yesterday. She was very helpful in suggesting that I own or accept as my own, the kindness of my peers' comments to me. She also offered a suggestion that what I was feeling as guilt – my reaction to when people express what they feel will be a loss – is really my overwhelming desire to contribute. She suggested that I look at my move as a decision to contribute elsewhere. It's strange to me that people describe me as being "the rock" or "the glue holding it all together." When all I want to do is be light, released, and non-sticky to connect with the ethereal. One of my managers said that I was like the "buffer" for everybody. I told him that my leaving was an opportunity for growth for everybody on my team. That a shift in process can be beneficial.

I had an interesting experience with Carl yesterday. I realize that this change is dramatic and the magnitude of it hasn't hit us completely yet. I had left my total compensation statement in the bathroom and Carl saw it this morning. He cursed when he saw that we'd lose the company's $6,000 contribution to my 401-K. Now I know he didn't intend for it to come out so harshly, but these kind of periodic bouts of truthfulness register deeply with me. I know that he's doing his best to be supportive, but occasionally his fear rises up and shows itself. He asked whether

I QUIT

there was anything my boss could do to help me keep it. It was like a desperation plea. It irritated me at first because I can still feel that fear. I do feel an inner calm, but I have to dig deeply.

1/20/02

On Friday I decided it would be a good thing to have some people over to celebrate my husband's birthday. It's tomorrow. There will be quite a crew with the kids included. I must remind myself not to limit my experience by the commitments I have for work. I must live in the moment, not looking at all of the things still to do beyond planning for this party. Right now I'm feeling a bit anxious about people feeling that I've left something incomplete. I suppose I'll ask my boss about her priorities again.

I feel "outed." Like I'm coming out of the closet. My closest friends have known my interests. My boss and I even talked about it two years ago. Being open about my interests has helped me to be to live more authentically. The most I've been in a long time and it brings me great peace. I remind myself that the truth is – there are no rules. We make them up, and so doing, limit ourselves. Like someone said we couldn't do it and then blame society for keeping us down. Hello! There are no rules! And any boundaries we experience we set up ourselves. So if you want to live in a "less than" scenario, just be responsible and acknowledge your choice in that. I'm not saying go out and do anything you want and be reckless (which is why responsibility is the third point in truth, self-trust/love, and responsibility) Be truthful and responsible. Be aware of the impact that your actions will have. Be loving in your gestures. Hold your loving intent in your heart, and others will be fine. Even if you separate from a personal relationship because you've realized that it's not serving you

Karyn Pettigrew

positively, if you hold the intention of doing what's right for you–without harm or malicious intent to another–ultimately the separation will benefit both. Paul Nunn helped characterize for me what I believe is true for all of us: "The world will benefit from me being the full expression of who I really am."

1/21/02

As my co-workers and I separate from each other, I can see how we worked with one another. I was too in the mix. I can see the "Karyn glue" that runs through the department. I am grateful for the time to wean ourselves properly. I can see how they will all grow when I'm gone. I can see how my level of involvement was perhaps stunting them and stressing me.

1/22/02

Every day it settles in a little more–ownership of my own power. The strength that lies in choosing to live outside the obvious–conventional wisdom. It amazes me how I speak to people of my decision. When people resonate with the content of my decision – abundance, passion, living more fully – or the action, the actual decision to go for it, their "good for you" or "I wish I could" comments humble me. I am keenly aware of how "different" or "out there" this decision may seem. The ones who think they know my family situation may say, "Oh well, I can see how she did it," and then rationalize why this kind of radical move is not for them. Except we never know another's true burdens– they don't know mine. I don't know theirs. But it doesn't matter because this process is for all of us. We may not be able to take two steps at a time, but the staircase is there.

Karyn Pettigrew   121

I QUIT

It's interesting to me, my reluctance to come out all the way and own up publicly that I want to help others heal. I won't call myself a healer while I acknowledge to myself that's all I want to do now. I'll call myself a teacher, guide, facilitator, not healer. Yet, I will allow myself the room to "get there one day," what I do and what it really is – helping others to heal – without taking stock of where I am now. What I do and what it really is – helping others to heal. Like it's some goal out there.

What comes with that is the notion of needing some formal training and another label that would authorize me to help others. So perhaps I won't call it healer, too much baggage. In fact, it doesn't really matter what I call myself. I know that a label can be misleading. We all have perceptions of what things mean. I guess what is most important is what the person I'm helping considers me – helper, guide, friend, counselor. Although sitting on my shoulder is the gentle reminder that others will need a reference. They'll want something to point to, to hang on to.

There's a part of me that wants a reference, too. I've been trained that way; every step thus far has been "legitimate." Cultivating the right labels to reduce the friction. "Don't challenge me, I'm a Harvard MBA with a Wellesley undergrad." I am ready to be in whatever is next for me, my adventure.

1/24/02

Even the weather beckons a change and reinforces the chaotic nature of life. It has been unseasonably warm – 50 today. Spring generally means starting anew. The momentary "spring" is symbolic to me, a reminder to start anew, be reborn.

I had lunch with a friend from the ad agency I worked with at my previous job. It was good to touch base; in a way it was like closure. I explained about my decision. He was aware of my "urban-spa" idea, but I elaborated on how it had morphed into a resource center for creating the life you really want. And then like so many others, we had an "aaahh" moment when the peace that comes with a move from the heart is internalized. When the person whom I'm talking to considers, for an instant, what that kind of freedom, authenticity would mean in his own life. Generally, it's fleeting. Some will say, "I wish I could do it." Sometimes it's just the silent stare of contemplation. And again I realize how important this work will be.

A co-worker stopped me in the hallway to wish me luck and express what a loss she thought my leaving would be for the organization. I expressed my gratitude at her taking the time to say so. I am honored and humbled by the support. I still feel a bit like I'm abandoning, particularly when they offer such sincere best wishes. It's like I'm watching myself through this process. It strengthens me, but it also challenges me to better understand, to see the bigger picture, and to go on.

I had my first big challenge today. The insurance guy called to say that the first company wouldn't even process the health-insurance application because of the Hodgkin's I had 20 years ago. I don't know how to tell my husband, except to tell him. I feel awful, but I'm angry, too–like I'm not supposed to follow my dream because this insurance company won't insure me. It's not right and I will trust. I'll go home, pray, meditate, and listen to my Donnie McClurkin track over and over until the negativity leaves me. Music, salve for the soul. Everyone should have at least one piece of music that carries them from this physical plane to that expanded place. So I must ask myself, and now what? I feel it will work out. I'll start by checking my Harvard directory to see if anyone is at the insurance company. Just keep pushing modestly. I trust that what I need most will be presented. I already have the insurance guy looking for another carrier. It will not end here.

1/26/02

I had a get together with friends from one of my metaphysics classes. It was good to see them and to speak about what's happening without the fear of being judged.

I was just thinking about sharing this experience with others, the idea of publishing one woman's experience with choosing to do what she felt in her heart.

2/2/02

I've been having thoughts about this writing and how it works for me, my stimulus for writing. And interestingly, I think of things in response to what I read or hear or catch on the TV or radio. I'm reading Sacred Contracts by Carolyn Myss and she just explained the history of one of her recurring dreams and its role in helping her to understand her path. It came to me, one of my recurring dream themes is what I call "catch me" dreams. Where I am with a group of friends and we are running away from something —monsters or something that we really don't see. We are running through apartment buildings, hotels, or towns, racing against the clock, trying to make it until morning. I somehow "know" the way and we instinctively go where I lead. We sometimes lose a few people, but many make it until morning. It makes me think of how I want to help lead people out of the maze of conventional life. The rat race against time we call our daily lives. Where something,

Karyn Pettigrew

monster/dark side, is chasing us, tracking us down. All we're trying to do is make it one more day. While in the dream I know how important it is to survive, I'm never deathly afraid, and I always make it.

2/04/02

It is an interesting time, as we get closer to my last day, everybody is really buckling down. It begins to descend into us centrally. My husband, while remaining fairly PC about it, focuses on his particular strength – responsibility in this physical realm–who, what, where, when, and how. I think he's right; he keeps me grounded. However, I still think he's getting nervous. He called me at work. I had to call him back, and he reminded me of the six figures that I make and that for the past six years we have really relied on my salary. That's all changing now, and he's shocked at how much money that has been. Which leads him to feel that we didn't put enough away. It's particularly easy to live up to your salary. The oddest thing is that I'm not panicked. I have faith without a perfectly clear plan. I have really good "paperwork," and I know that I can find a job if I need to. I think that my composure is the result of feeling secure in my capabilities and knowing that I can always "retreat."

2/5/02

It's been a series of ups and downs. In a way it feels like a bereavement process. I wake up and realize how "out there" I am. This is the first time in my life that I didn't have the "next step" all figured out, for the bigger title, more money, ascension. And yet, perhaps that's exactly what is happening in a non-material way. A bigger title may be equal to a better knowledge of me. More money may be equivalent to greater gratification and payoff because I'm living in my passion zone. I am acutely aware that I have to be gentle with my husband because to a certain extent, he's swimming in the backwash of my decision. I have to remember that this is a co-creative process and that his head is not where mine is on this. Could it be that I am avoiding reality under the "faith" that the Universe will meet me half-way? Am I delusional?

This morning my husband declared that our situation was bleak. And not so kindly, I said, "Bleak is an attitude. The situation is what it is." He said, "Oh, brother, I can't talk to you about this..." I responded with, "If we consider it bleak, it will be. We have to see it as it is and then choose to make changes that will be more in line with what we want." In a way, it awakened us to how loosely we had been living – not extravagantly or wastefully, but comfortably and unconsciously. There are those who live with less than we, but are more fulfilled. He agreed. I wasn't going after a "win" with him. I suppose that my fear about this move rises to the surface when the physical practicalities are thrown at me. I do believe that there is a creative solution for everything.

2/6/02

I had a conversation with a retiring manager at the company today. I explained what I was planning to do and he exhaled. He went on to explain his torment in deciding to retire. How the stress had begun to take its toll on him physically. He had been at the company 24 years and did not feel recognized for his contribution in the end. He had had ulcers for the past five years along with other physical ailments, such that he finally said enough. He was also sad because they were dismantling his department. He feels that his life's work is being broken apart without pause or thanks. He was having trouble because as he said, "this is who I am." But I said to him today and will shout from the rooftops going forward, "The job is not who you are; It's what you do today! It's the context for you to be who you are." Who he is can go anywhere; it travels with him.

The president of the utility stopped by to wish me well and to say thanks. It meant a lot to me. I really appreciated it. I still care, although I know I'm just one person in this huge organization and easily replaceable. And so while I try to learn to live beyond the external validation, not thinking about what others think, I still do. Will I reach the point where I don't think about, and therefore don't need, the external validation?

2/11/02

I'm three weeks away from my last day. I attended a lecture with one of my former students and we started talking about how I had felt one time that I needed to be seen and accepted at work as "right." What was I looking for? My voice? Confirmation that I was right? I know now that finding my voice ts not about someone else seeing me as right. The point is that no one else can validate me, but me. Any expectation that I would one day be held up and praised for being right, would have led to a great deal of disappointment. The real assertive power was in choosing to do what I did, in spite of what others might think.

2/18/02

We are headed home from our ski trip tomorrow. It was a good trip, albeit filled with work distractions for me. I haven't been able to stop thinking about work, particularly unfinished pieces.

I QUIT

Intellectually, I realize that it will never be "finished." But, of course, I want everything in "lock down," planned out. The reality is that the place will be different, with different people making decisions and recommendations. They need to come to them on their own. Trust their own decision-making abilities. I can't plan out how they'll get there beyond the template that I've laid out. They must grow into the open spaces and fill them up with their insights and direction. I find that my separation blues remain most significantly linked to my boss of eight years. She has been a major influence in my life. It's a bit like leaving home for the first time.

I continue to get synchronistic messages that keep me focused and more secure as my corporate days evaporate. Another parent at my daughter's school relayed the story of her life-altering visit to a homeopath. Some people are amazed that I was so involved in this alternative medicine thing and so effective at work. I am awed by the potential accomplishments if I focus my head and heart in the same direction. How many people will themselves to success? How many feel empty despite the normal accoutrements of success? I realize that no matter what I do, how hard I work, someone else may not feel that it's good enough. Can they take away what matters most – honor, integrity, truth, love, and responsibility? No. To believe falsely in anyone's power over me is my greatest mistake. This is the last and hardest part of unplugging from external validation. And it's indeed very difficult. It has been the hardest thing I've ever done. I've left three other jobs in my life, but always to pursue greater levels of the same – status, power, money, personal connections. I wonder, if in six months, I'll look back and wince at how wound up I've been. I recognize that I have to let go of what's in my hand to reach for the next thing. I don't know what is around the corner.

Karyn Pettigrew

2/28/02

I feel guilty about how happy I am that I'm leaving, so I reserve demonstration of my exuberance. I think that its hard for my staff. They're a bit afraid of relying on themselves, but I know that experience is the best teacher, and not until I'm gone will they really kick into gear.

3/6/02

It's been much too long since I last wrote. During my meditation, I received guidance that I needed to let go. My old identity was dead and a new one was ready to emerge. I am in the midst of a grieving process for the old me. I know it, feel it, and don't care for it much. I was very tied into my old job. I laughingly call it detoxing, but I'ts more about finding my center, self-esteem from my center. I acknowledge that I expect a shoe to drop, for something to be wrong at the job. Logically, it is highly unlikely.

I wrote a thank you/ forgiveness note. I acknowledged all of the value that my life's experiences bring to bear on the new life, and then I went outside and burned it.

-THE END-

FOOTNOTES

1. The Popcorn Report "CASHING OUT" Emerging Trend.

2. Jon Kabat-Zinn, Wherever you go–Ter you are, p. 206, Hyperion 1994

3. Sarah Ban Breathnach, Something More, p. 133, Time-Warner 1998

4. Laws of Spirit, Dan Millman, 1995 HJ Kramer Book, p. 39

5. The Columbia Encyclopedia, Sixth Edition. 2001

6. www.workinamerica.org, Holding a Job, Having a Life: Stratigies for Change

Ms. Pettigrew received her Bachelor of Arts degree in Ecomonics from Wellesley College and her Masters of Business Administration degree from Harvard University. She has been facilitating courses on creative manifestation and work/life balance for the past several years. Ms. Pettigrew currently sees clients for private consultations and corporate consulting.

For more information about Karyn Pettigrew's workshops, lectures,coaching and consulting call 773-233-9214 or email Karyn@kpconsulting.biz